DATE DUE

DEC 2 2			
MY 09 '06			
GAYLORD			PRINTED IN U.S A.

THE LONELY HEROES: PROFESSIONAL BASKETBALL'S GREAT CENTERS

Other books by Merv Harris:
On Court with the Superstars of the NBA (editor)
The Fabulous Lakers

THE LONELY HEROES: PROFESSIONAL BASKETBALL'S GREAT CENTERS

MERV HARRIS

The Viking Press   New York

First published in 1975 by The Viking Press, Inc.
625 Madison Avenue, New York, N.Y. 10022
Published simultaneously in Canada by
The Macmillan Company of Canada Limited

LIBRARY OF CONGRESS CATALOGING IN PUBLICATION DATA
Harris, Merv.
    The lonely heroes.
    1. Basketball—Biography. I. Title.
GV884.A1H35   796.32'3'0922 [B]   75-8977
ISBN 0-670-43764-6

Printed in U.S.A.

Unless otherwise specified the photographs are by Walter Iooss, Jr.

For Morris and Sara Harris, whose love started things,
and for Ira Walsh, whose shoving, shouting,
and prodding kept them moving

CONTENTS

THE LONELY HEROES: PROFESSIONAL BASKETBALL'S GREAT CENTERS

1

A GAME FOR TALL, TALL MEN

Wilt Chamberlain rose from the well-worn bench in front of his locker in the functionally austere shower and dressing room of the Loyola University men's gymnasium in Los Angeles. He wore only a jock strap, and his muscles rippled with suppressed power as he strode across the long, concrete-floored room. From 20 feet away, he was a big, muscular man. From 15 feet away, he was huge . . . awesome. From 10 feet away, he seemed to be obliterating everything from sight. And, when he came within arm's length to reach for the pen I offered him, I felt . . . for the first time in my life . . . dwarfed—absolutely overwhelmed, a gnat in the presence of this vast human being, and I repressed a shudder at the realization of his size and strength.

I gave a brief, silent thanks my mission with him was trivial and quickly accomplished. I shuddered at the thought of the havoc he might create had he been striding toward me in anger rather than simply to sign a roster sheet. He was to indicate his preference for a token gift for appearing in the 1963 National Basketball Association All-Star Game to be played the next evening at the Los Angeles Sports Arena.

It was a brief, insignificant moment for Wilt Chamberlain among the thousands of insignificant moments which have been part of his career in sports. I was in the locker room to interview players for my story in the next day's Los Angeles *Herald-Examiner* and, as a favor to the Los Angeles Lakers' management, which was conducting the game, to get each player's choice of gift while I was there.

I'd not thought much about size those three years since the Lakers had introduced pro basketball to the West Coast. The players were big . . . but so was I, relatively speaking, and so what? I'd seen Chamberlain. I'd seen Bill Russell. And I'd seen the other big men who played in the league. I'd interviewed them after games. I liked the people who played pro basketball, I liked writing stories about them, and I liked writing stories about their game.

The impact of their size simply hadn't registered fully until Chamberlain strode toward me that afternoon in mid-January of 1963 and towered above me. In that moment, somehow, the story my grandfather had related to me many, many years before . . . the Old Testament story of David and the fearsome Goliath . . . had an impact and meaning I'd failed to grasp, really, as I sat there, a boy at an old man's knee. Now, I felt what *giant* truly meant. And I marveled with sudden new insight at the bravery of the shepherd boy who'd faced the mighty warrior of the Philistines armed only with his sling.

Wilt Chamberlain was a friend. Had he been my enemy, I'd not dare to confront him with anything less than a howitzer.

/ / /

Abnormal size and strength brand men freaks as much today as in Biblical times. Giants have been assigned roles throughout history as warriors or as amusements—always a breed apart and either to be feared or mocked, seldom to be recognized as capable of the warm, subtle emotions taken for granted as attributes of "normal" people.

Giants, painted often as crude and brutal, are objects of ridicule equally in the legends of the earth's most primitive peoples and in the great literature of contemporary civilization. Almost always, giants are undone—because their muscles are no match for smaller men's cunning and because their size makes them vulnerable to those with wit and courage.

"Fee, fi, fo fum," rumbles the dull-minded Giant. "Whack, whack, whack," sings Jack's ax as he chops down the bean stalk and sends the Giant crashing to ignoble death. "Tell me again about the rabbits," pleads the huge Lenny to sly little George in Steinbeck's *Of Mice and Men*.

/ / /

The cultural gap from nursery tale to contemporary classic is huge, yet the theme is constant: giant equals stupid, small equals smart. It is always open season on the big man. He is fair game for practical jokes and cruel badgering. "How's the weather up there?" asks the country sharpie of the side-show giant. And the giant glowers in impotent silence on his rickety platform as the rustic's buddies chuckle at their daring companion's wit.

The tools and structures of society are designed for beings six feet tall, give or take an inch or three. Doorways and room ceilings and clothing and mirrors and elevators and beds and scissors and knives and forks and airplane seats and shower heads and automobiles and shopping carts and school desks and thousands of other things taken for granted as part of

Seven-foot Wilt Chamberlain overlooks a sea of news media faces in Los Angeles Lakers locker room during 1972–73 NBA playoffs

daily living . . . these things are Everyman's. For the giant, tools and clothing and travel and even the simple repose of slumber present special problems requiring pains and precautions which make life for him a constant harangue. And, rather than offering help or understanding to his out-sized brother, Everyman stands aside to snicker at his predicament.

"If I were given a change of life," admitted Wilt Chamberlain once, exposing his and probably all giants' yearnings, "I'd like to see how it would be to live as a mere six-footer, so I could get the perspective of looking at the world, and particularly at people, at another level. I can remember always being taller than anyone else, and I'd like to face people without their being affected or intimidated by physical stature."

He stands seven feet, one and one-sixteenth inches tall. By his own measure. And he weighs, depending on the season and the current activity commanding his attention, close to 300 pounds. He is a millionaire. He is black. He is a fascinating and complex man. Born 2000 years ago, he might have become an indentured foot soldier in a Roman legion or a freak on display in a province-touring circus. He might have been scorned and alone. Born, as he was, in contemporary America, he is a celebrity. He has been permitted a special role in our society because we offer at least one haven and accommodation for the giant: We seek him out, offer him riches, and then demand of him great accomplishments in the special world of basketball. We must have our games, and here is one which not only permits, but actually demands, exceptional height.

/ / /

A game invented in 1891 to provide wintertime exercise for a college gym class has become, in our time, a sanctuary for the giant and a means for him to become rich.

The concept of basketball, reduced to simplest terms, is to propel an inflated rubber ball approximately 12 inches in diameter through a ring 18 inches in diameter and suspended 10 feet in the air. Alone among our popular professional sports, basketball is played in a vertical rather than horizontal space and thus, uniquely, it is a game offering special opportunity for tall, tall men.

A football team traverses 100 yards from one end of the

field to the other to record its scores. In basketball, in contrast, the move of 94 feet from one goal area to the other is valueless until the ball is elevated 10 feet from playing surface to, and then through, the hoop.

Another original concept of basketball was that it should be a noncontact sport. Dr. James Naismith chose an elevated goal for just this reason, in fact, and the 10-foot height was determined—in an era during which average American height was well under six feet—because that was the clearance of a running track around the gym floor at the YMCA teacher's training college at Springfield, Massachusetts. Two peach baskets were suspended from the rim of the track to provide the goals for the first game . . . and heaving a soccer ball into those baskets was no simple feat.

The closer a man could get first to the area under the basket, then up into the vertical space directly below it, the easier scoring goals became. An exceptionally tall man—who could first position himself directly under the basket, then could reach up to put the ball through the hoop with minimum jump—had a major advantage over shorter players. To minimize that advantage, the shorter men could attempt physically to prevent the big man from getting original position close to the basket . . . to the degree that officials sanctioned pushing and shoving, that is.

And thus, even within the first, early months of the sport's mushrooming popularity, playing patterns were established that have been characteristics of the game ever since.

In a still-continuing process of rules evolvement, three sets of factors have always been involved.

First, there had to be safeguards for players' physical safety. Some pushing and shoving and hitting would always be part of the game, because it is played by competitive people, but there must be a stopping-point short of mayhem.

Second, it has had to be recognized that basketball is a ticket-selling enterprise. When the professional league introduced the 24-second rule in 1954 to prevent stalling and lack of action, the motivation was economic survival—the crowd-pleasing appeal of enforced, fast-paced action—much more than concern for the purity of the game.

Third, there has been a constant attempt to provide relative balance in basketball between offense and defense so that there would always be relative parity between the two phases of the game. In practice, this third major pattern in rules has usually been to invoke new restrictions against the men vertically closest to the goal—the giants.

In earliest basketball, the biggest man on a team could station himself near the basket, wait for his smaller teammates to pass the ball to him, then turn with a slight jump and score his relatively easy field goal. In an early attempt to restore balance between this stationary big man and those attempting to restrict him, a zone was established which was six feet across and within whose keyhole-shaped boundary no player could remain for more than three seconds.

The effect was to minimize the advantage for the big man-based offense over a defense. A secondary effect was to encourage bigger men to become more agile so that they could set their position, receive a pass, and score their field goals all within the mandatory three-second period.

Until 1937, the two centers lined up after every goal to resume play by a tossup of the ball between them—the *center jump.* The center who consistently could outjump his rival and get the ball to his teammates was a prize indeed. Later, the tipoff was restricted to openings of each quarter or half. The center's value to his team became a bit less than it had been before, but defenses against big men became more sophisticated, too, and the talented center continued to be a winning team's greatest asset.

In that era, a man as small as 5-foot-4 or as small as a 5-foot-10 Purdue University All-American named John Wooden, for example, had no inherent incapability of reaching stardom within the relatively little-publicized world of basketball as it was played at the time. A height of 6 feet or more was ample for a man playing the forward position, and there was no effective minimum height for the ball-handlers and playmakers who worked at guard. A 6-foot-2 center was the rule and the player 6-foot-6 or taller, with mobility, the rarity.

There were people in America who soared above and beyond the 7-foot mark, of course, just as there had always been in history. Most of them were endowed with their size not through the good fortune of genetic inheritance and good nutrition, but through malfunction of the gland—the pituitary—which controls human growth.

The *pituitary giant* is characterized by elongated legs and arms in proportion to his trunk, and tends to be massive and painfully, self-consciously awkward. He is often susceptible to illness. Afflicted with all the japes and problems society imposes upon the outsized, the pituitary giant is seldom interested in basketball.

A different type of giant, normally proportioned, is what medical men call the *inherent giant*—well muscled, well coordinated, exceptionally well endowed genetically through parents and grandparents generally of unusual height themselves. Wilt Chamberlain, Bill Russell and—today—most of the men who play professional basketball are *inherent,* rather than *pituitary,* giants.

There were few men of 6-foot-8, 6-foot-9, or more playing basketball in its earlier days because statistically they were so few within the over-all national population, let alone within basketball. With improved medical treatment for expectant mothers, improved pediatric medicine, improved national nutrition, improved recreational and physical education opportunities within the past two decades, the national health picture has advanced so startlingly that volumes of statistics support the claim that America is a land of people bigger and healthier than they were only one or two generations ago.

/ / /

The law of supply and demand works as forcefully in athletics as it does in other areas of commerce.

Crude petroleum seeping upward through the earth was a nuisance to farmers until the invention and then the zooming popularity of the motorcar. Ultimately, there was a scarcity of petroleum. And with scarcity came a skyrocketing of cost.

Giants were too awkward and too immobile for baseball, soccer, gymnastics, and other sports. Then came basketball. Opportunity developed. In our era, as basketball came to be a major professional spectator sport, giants became a desperate necessity in order for a team to succeed. And thus the giant—if he was good enough—commanded huge sums of money.

A survey conducted by sportswriter Leonard Koppett of *The New York Times* in the spring of 1973 found that professional basketball players' incomes were substantially greater, on the average, than incomes for baseball, football, and hockey players. Fully 45 per cent of the National Basketball Association teams' gross incomes, or about $18 million, went into salaries, Koppett found, while the American Basketball Association devoted 32 per cent of income to salaries in contrast to major league baseball's 17 per cent of a $130-million income. By agreement between the league and respective players' associations, no NBA or ABA player could be paid less than $17,500 per season, whereas a National Football League team could pay a man as little as $12,000.

Koppett estimated that among 1040 National Football League players in 1972, only 10 received a salary as great as $100,000 per season. Thirty of 600 major league baseball players earned at least $100,000, or 5 per cent, but there were 15 of 120 ABA men at $100,000 (13 per cent), and an astounding 50 of 204 NBA men (25 per cent) earned at least that sum.

One aspect of this lofty salary range for basketball players, in contrast to the two other major national spectator sports, is that while baseball and football leagues are unified under common managements, pro basketball has been split since 1967 between warring leagues, each bidding for talent independently without the money-saving advantages of common free-agent drafts.

However, the scarcity of extremely tall men unquestionably has compounded the basketball leagues' talent problems and, clearly, the law of supply and demand has put a premium on rangy, mobile seven-footers. It is a seller's rather than buyer's market.

A basketball player is drafted, and then a bidding war begins. Athletes' well-rewarded agents bargain for high bonuses for the players' original agreements with teams. He demands for the player a salary beyond $200,000 a year. He demands annual salary payments on a deferred basis after the player's retirement to minimize any one year's tax bite. And the agent seeks fringe benefits such as special-performance bonuses or low-interest, long-term loans to be used for investments and tax shelters.

Before a player even gets to the complicated bargaining of

pro basketball, he is pursued and wooed by as many as 200 or 300 colleges anxious to recruit him as he prepares to leave high school. Often a player has even been eagerly recruited by high-school coaches as he reaches young manhood out of junior high. Academic capability or potential is given scant consideration as coaches and alumni visualize championships an outstanding player may represent.

This bitterly competitive system tends to breed a group of pampered and privileged young men who are self-conscious and gaped at for their extreme height in most of their day-to-day public activities, yet applauded and idolized in one specific (perhaps trivial in their own view) activity—basketball. Only a strong, self-assured personality can survive such contrasting and conflicting treatments. Few gawky, impoverished, ghetto-bred adolescents possess that kind of inner stability.

When one of basketball's all-time playing stars, Bob Cousy, resigned bitterly in December of 1973 as coach of the NBA's Kansas City–Omaha Kings, he decried the system that produces such warped young men and which makes coaching them so difficult. At "only" 6-foot-3 regarded, of all things, as one of the sport's all-time best "little men," Cousy looked back at a thirteen-year playing career, at nearly six years as coach at Boston College, and then at five years in professional coaching, to admit, "I'm fed up with the whole thing. This has been building for a long time. There's more to life than winning and losing basketball games. My feelings about basketball haven't changed *per se,* but the system as it stands today has created monsters—athletes who are spoiled from the time they get out of grammar school. I just reached a point where I could make a choice of coaching or not coaching for more aesthetic reasons than money.

"It's this grotesque overemphasis on winning. It's a value system gone astray.

"The same situation exists to a degree in other sports, but it's more flagrant in basketball. It starts with the recruiting system spoiling the kids so badly. They're pampered and catered to from the time they're playground players. They have an exaggerated opinion of their role in society. They expect instant recognition, exposure, and financial rewards while men are going to the moon, doctors are working on cancer cures, and others are spending their lives trying to effect meaningful changes. Then, when they get to be pros, the inflated salaries make them instant millionaires. As a coach, you're supposed to mold ten or twelve of these into a cohesive unit. Logically, it can't be done. I think it's a shame.

"There's a great deal of money at stake in college basketball. Recruiting starts the whole vicious circle. Naturally, the athletes take advantage. Hell, any of us would do the same thing."

Larry Costello, a contemporary of Cousy's as a 6-foot backcourt player in pro basketball's pioneering days and since 1968 coach of the Milwaukee Bucks, pinpoints another aspect of the problems which, Cousy says, drove him out of the league. "I don't think the NBA puts out the best basketball it could," Costello said. "There are just too many teams and too many players. What I'd like to see is about fourteen teams in just one league. Then the fans would see good basketball night in and night out.

"Players don't have to be hungry any more to get a job. With all the teams around, if a guy gets cut, he can probably latch on with another club if he has any talent at all. If you had fourteen teams you'd have about a hundred and forty players—good players. A guy would know that he'd have to bust his rear every night just to keep his job."

Wooed by high salaries, goaded thereafter into polishing their physical skills, pushed and pulled by external and internal conflicts and ambitions, the basketball player faces pressures which cannot but distort and harden. A Wilt Chamberlain retires to the self-indulgent luxury of a multi-million-dollar mansion, flaunts his flamboyance, and lives like an Oriental potentate. A Bill Russell undergoes a change of life style from married life in a Boston suburb to the tinsel of Hollywood show-business semibachelorhood and back to orthodoxy as coach of a professional team in staid Seattle. An Elvin Hayes gropes for stability and finds it in Pentecostal Christianity. A Lew Alcindor searches for meaning and identity and emerges as Kareem Abdul-Jabbar, devout and obedient servant of Allah. . . .

Basketball's gaints are among our greatest heroes. We marvel at their physical majesty as they soar high above the playing floor to slam balls through the basket or reach for a rebound. We revel when their skills bring victories to our teams.

Yet the giant, simply by his existence, goads us that we are puny in his presence, impotent in our insignificance in implied potential combat. We compete with the giant by meeting him with ridicule.

In the conflicts and dramas of professional basketball, the giant comes into his own. He is mighty and he is magnificent in triumph, but his humiliation is all the greater in defeat.

The giant is *of* man, but apart from man . . . splendid, but perpetually in splendid isolation, too.

2

THE CACKLING GENIUS:
BILL RUSSELL

It was a relatively meaningless early-season game in December 1965. Cold, dirty Eastern-city snow fell in depressing billows outside the huge old brick building which housed not only a venerable athletic arena called Boston Garden, but also the North Station commuter-train depot. Less than 6000 fans cared to venture out into the cold, even though the opponents in that night's National Basketball Association game were the world champion Boston Celtics and their perennial title-series victims, the Los Angeles Lakers.

Los Angeles was clinging precariously to first place in the Western Division, having lost its last three games. The Celtics were in their accustomed first-place position in the East and seemed, as early as that December 8, certain to be playoff finalists once again.

But a gawky, tangle-footed youngster named Mel Counts played at center for the Celtics that night, as he had for the past three games, and the Boston team could not assert itself as it usually did. The pace was plodding and first the Lakers would score, then the Celtics. With two minutes left in the third period, the Lakers put together a mild string of points and led for the first time, 85-81. Time out was called.

The Lakers bounced off the court and clustered around

their coach, clapping hands energetically and yapping encouragements at each other.

The Celtics came to their bench more casually. Less was at stake for them than for the Lakers, and the relative insignificance of the game made Boston's lethargy understandable.

At the end of the Celtic bench, there suddenly arose a commotion. He had been a spectator for the three preceding games and for all of this one, yards of tape wrapped around his right thigh to promote healing in a pulled hamstring muscle. Now Bill Russell could sit no more. Stoop-shouldered, almost shambling in his gait, and with his leg swaddled in bandages, Russell limped over to confer with a pudgy, russet-haired, balding man named Arnold Auerbach. The coach.

The gaunt, straggle-bearded 6-foot-9¾-inch black man and the small, angry-looking white man jawed at each other for a moment, and then Auerbach nodded in assent. Russell hobbled over to the scorer's table to report, flung his green Celtic's warmup jacket to a ballboy, and, when the referee whistled the teams back onto the floor, it was Russell stationed in the middle of the Boston lineup, not Counts.

A Laker converted a pair of free throws and Los Angeles' lead was 87-81. Russell stepped behind the basket to in-bounds the ball. He spotted a teammate far down court, passed to him for a quick field goal.

The Lakers brought the ball upcourt now, but Jerry West missed from 18 feet. Russell dipped on that bad leg, leaped off of it to grab the rebound away from a pair of slower-to-react Lakers. He passed in the same motion to K. C. Jones, and the Celtics' guard sprinted down the middle of the court to score another easy field goal as three green-shirted Boston players converged on just two blue-shirted Los Angeles defenders.

Upcourt came the Lakers again, their earlier vigor deserting them. Darrall Imhoff, the Los Angeles center, tried his left-handed jumper from 14 feet as Russell lay back from him, protecting the area under the basket. The shot clunked off the rim and headed for the corner. Russell leaped for it, grabbed it, once again passed to K. C., and the Celtics had another fast break—three-on-one this time. The score was tied.

The three-quarter mark passed in the game with the score

knotted, and the once stodgy pace accelerated to rapid bursts of running. The Celtics often managed to get outnumbering situations off their Russell-ignited fast breaks and scored, when they scored, on layup shots from point-blank range. The Lakers were methodical . . . because they had little choice. When Los Angeles tried to shoot, the ranges were 14 to 20 feet or more. Once, when West managed to snake past the outer perimeter of defense, he attempted a layup of his own, only to have Russell leap at him in two vast, quick strides from 10 feet away and bat the ball out of the air before it could begin its downward trajectory.

At the final buzzer, the Celtics were the winners, 108-106, and Russell had managed 10 rebounds along with three blocked shots. He had played only 14 minutes and hadn't scored a point. Yet he was clearly the hero of the night.

At game's end, his shoulders stooped again and his gait fell at once from sprinter pace to pained limp as he retreated into his team's locker room.

"I asked Red [Coach Auerbach] if I could go in," Russell explained. Reporters clustered around him had pressed him for an explanation—why he had risked long-time reinjury in an early-season game—and he'd only reluctantly complied.

"What made you decide to play?" I asked.

The reply was terse: "Winning the game."

The man who had led the Celtics, at that point, to seven consecutive NBA championships leaned back on the bench. Gingerly he unwrapped the layers of tape from his thigh. He probed gently with a bony finger, wincing at the pain.

"I figured if I was careful, I might not pull it too bad," he said. "Still, I did hurt it . . . but we've got a few days off to treat it."

"Did the hamstring pull bother you out there?"

Again a crisp, wincing reply. "It was hurting."

Now Russell became self-conscious. Other Celtics had taken part in the victory, but only he was being interviewed. He rose, terminating the questioning. "It ain't no big deal," he snapped impatiently, "Hell, we're pros."

/ / /

Today, his once painfully gaunt frame padded with 20 or 30 retirement-brought pounds, Bill Russell serves as coach of

His thigh bandaged to protect a muscle pull, Boston's Bill Russell reaches toward Boston Gardens rafters to swat down field-goal attempt by Los Angeles' Gail Goodrich. Fluttering banners represent incredible succession of championships won by Celtics in Russell's career

the Seattle Sonics. Younger fans know him as the mod-garbed Seattle coach or as an acid-tongued, cackling-laughing "color man" for Game of the Week national telecasts.

As a player, Bill Russell was the most revolutionary figure in the history of the game. He *invented* the contemporary style of center position play and, less directly, *invented* the fast-paced, all-out-action style of play which has made pro basketball one of the nation's fastest-growing sports.

That December 8, 1965, game was just one of many in which I saw Russell play against the Lakers, but it stands clearly in memory because it incorporated in so many different ways the tangible and intangible contributions Russell made to the Celtics as they established the greatest record of accomplishment in pro sports history—11 championships in the 13 seasons between 1957 and 1969, the last two with Russell the player-coach . . . first black coach in NBA history.

Russell's on-court intensity and concentration were major factors in his and his team's success. Although a giant, he was quick-handed and quick-footed in his movements. He domi-nated every game in which he played. He controlled the rebounding. He was the hub for the Celtics' simple, but effective, set-play offense. He was the center of the Celtics' aggressive defense. And he was a man capable of rising some-how to the need of the moment, seemingly willing to make any personal sacrifice required for his team to achieve victory.

This was one aspect of the complex Russell personality . . . Russell the athlete.

He was a product of black, rural Monroe, Louisiana, and later of the Oakland, California, black ghetto. He was a man who suffered indignities often in his early life, he said, because he was black. Giving himself and his life perspective, Russell could say, too, "I don't consider anything I have done as contributing to society. I consider playing professional basket-ball as marking time, the most shallow thing in the world."

He refused once to play in a game in Lexington, Kentucky, because he and his black teammates were refused service at their hotel coffee shop. He was fined by the NBA office another time for protesting bitterly—and accurately—that the league had established an unwritten, but observed, "quota" on the number of blacks retained on a team's roster. He refuses, to this day, to sign autographs because he consid-ers this ritual of athletic adulation a mere triviality. And, in 1975, he spurned admission to the basketball Hall of Fame for reasons he refused to discuss.

The civil-rights movement and the era of militant black self-assertion have worked a revolution in the land within the span of a single generation—Russell's generation. In his way, Rus-sell was a pioneer and a leader. Assertion of black masculinity through hairdo and beards and mustaches and striking cloth-ing are aspects of society accepted today without question. When Russell grew a mustache and goatee more than a decade ago, he branded himself a freak, an unregenerate rebel.

"I've thought about it and I've thought about it," Russell admitted in 1963. "Why did I wear the beard? It's part of this thing—I've always fought so hard to be different and I am different without even trying, and maybe it's just my own little revolution. It just isn't done in polite circles, in a sense. But I do think it's part of my personality. When I first joined the Celtics, I shaved the beard off. I did it on my own. It was none of their business, and if I had valued their opinion I would have asked them. I made a concession to conformity at that time. Then I grew it back. After we won the first championship, I let [teammate Tom] Heinsohn shave it off, and then I grew it back again. It was a very childish thing, in the sense of defiance.

"I wear it now to let people know that I am an individual. I do think for myself, and I'm very opinionated. Contrary to popular belief, I'm a living, thinking, breathing human being."

This kind of fierce integrity is often reflected in things Russell has said and done during his playing career, in the interim period following his retirement from the Celtics in 1969, and since then in his return to the NBA as a coach. "They say I owe the public *this* and I owe the public *that*," he said. "What I owe the public is the best performance I can give, *period*."

/ / /

Had Russell grown up in luxury and acclaim, perhaps he'd not have established the values of self-assertion and candor which became his trademarks as an athlete and as a man. It was not until his freshman year at the University of San Francisco that his body began to fill up as well as out. His special contribution to basketball came not as a positive thing, really, but, rather, his emphasis on defense and his uncanny shot-blocking abilities developed as his way of compensating for skills he lacked.

"When I got out of high school, I was six-five and weighed one hundred and fifty-eight pounds. A real mass of muscles," Russell recalled once, cackling in that braying, piercing laugh which is as much his trademark as his beard.

Wiry, gawky, younger brother of an outstanding athlete, Russell was self-conscious as a boy. He failed in a tryout for the McClymonds High School football team and then managed only to be player number 15½ on a 16-man junior varsity basketball team at 6-foot-3. There were 15 uniforms available and Russell alternated with a youngster named Roland Campbell wearing that last sub's outfit. As a 6-foot-4 high-school junior, Russell made the varsity—but seldom got into games. Finally, as a senior, Russell became the starter. The team would go on to win the Oakland prep championship, but Russell graduated in mid-season and he was not the star. In his best game he scored only 14 points.

To excite the basketball world of 20 years ago, a center had to be a scorer. The model was the great, massive George Mikan of the pro Minneapolis Lakers, voted basketball's greatest player of the half century. George would lumber down the court, establish his offensive position near the basket, receive passes lobbed at him from the outside, and then would turn powerfully to the basket. Using his left arm like a club, Mikan swept people out of his way to score virtually at will with his right-handed hook shots from short range. It was a power game, an offensive game.

Russell, slender, ill equipped to overpower opponents, and not yet exceptionally tall, learned in countless practice hours and boys' club pickup games that he could contribute to McClymonds High's success by substituting leaping ability and quickness for power and high scoring. He didn't manufacture many points himself, but he developed a knack for keeping the other team from scoring. He could play deep, near the basket, and leap up and out to block opponents' field-goal attempts. His movements were crude, at that, but it was his way and it established Russell's style on the basketball court as clearly as a shy wit was beginning to establish him as a rare individual.

There were no scholarship offers tempting Russell as he neared graduation from McClymonds in January 1953. Bob Feerick, a former pro all-star from the pioneer days of the NBA who, today, is an executive with the Golden State Warriors, coached at the time at the University of Santa Clara.

Warming up for 1956 Olympic Games in
Melbourne, two-time All-American Bill
Russell of USF demonstrates the back-
ward, two-handed stuff

Feerick recruited competitively against nearly a dozen Bay Area colleges playing top-level basketball. He looked back to 1953 to recall, "We didn't think much about Russell. He was a kid over at McClymonds. He was small. He was nothing. He grew up *after* he got to college."

In Russell's last high-school game, he was seen by Hal DeJulio, an assistant coach at the University of San Francisco. USF had emerged from obscurity in 1949 to win the National Invitational Tournament at Madison Square Garden under Coach Pete Newell, but the Jesuit-supported mid-city school had no campus gym of its own and had returned to only regional importance under Coach Phil Woolpert. DeJulio, a member of the '49 team, saw something in the 6-foot-5 youngster's aggressiveness and his way of blocking shots which suggested, somehow, he might be an effective player in Woolpert's defense-stressing, ball-control style. At DeJulio's urging, Russell was offered a scholarship.

Woolpert was intense and ambitious. His West Coast-instilled ideas of basketball demanded methodical, intricate, patterned offense and grinding, dogged, man-to-man defense. Today, he lives happily in semiretirement in the evergreen forests of the State of Washington. On a visit to San Francisco in the fall of 1973, Woolpert remembered, "I didn't teach Bill his style of defense—he brought it with him. All I taught him—and all my assistants taught him, really—was to keep his knees flexed . . . which I consider the key to good defense."

/ / /

Relations between the coach and the player were not tranquil. Woolpert did not readily grasp the impact of Russell's special capabilities and Russell was still too young, too uncertain of himself socially as he emerged from Oakland to assert himself too strongly as an individual. In time, working with assistant coaches DeJulio and Ross Giudice and with an older player, a guard named K. C. Jones, Russell polished a set of tactics and techniques which opened a new era in basketball.

Russell's mental and physical quickness enabled him to do more than his first responsibility, which was simply to guard the opposing center. Russell could handle this orthodox man-to-man assignment, but he could also react quickly to another man's moving past a USF defender and attacking the basket.

Should an opponent drive around a USF guard and head for the hoop, for example, he'd find Russell striding toward him to leap up and block the shot. Another time, the opponent might whip the USF player again, drive to the basket, hesitate a moment looking for Russell to block him . . . and not find Russell, but miss the shot anyway because his concentration waivered.

It was a devastating refutation to a number of offensive and defensive ideas which, until Russell's time, had been as ingrained in basketball as the Ten Commandments were supposed to be in everyday life.

In the fundamental, one-on-one confrontation in basketball between individual defender and individual offensive player, it had always been the option of the man with the ball to attempt either to shoot from distances away from the basket or, instead, to dribble past the defender and drive to the basket for a layup. Slow-footed defenders were handicapped because they could be outraced and victimized for layups. A response for Mr. Slow would be to play back, away from his man, so he could not be beaten . . . even though this tactic made Mr. Quick's outside shot that much easier to launch. The closer a defender played to the offensive player, the better the likelihood of preventing the outside shot, but at the risk of the offensive player's taking a quick step past the defender and being free for a drive to the hoop.

Russell's ability to move away from his own man and to protect against the offensive players' attempted layups unbalanced an offensive-defensive relationship which, until then, was unquestioned. With Russell, the USF defenders could keep as close to offensive players as they chose to be. They could defend primarily against the outside shot, knowing Russell would "pick up the loose cutter," to use the basketball jargon, if they were beaten. The offensive player lost his advantage of initiative and option. He could no longer make the USF defender guess whether he'd try the outside shot or the layup.

Years later, what Russell could do for a defensively feeble

teammate was laughingly institutionalized among the Boston Celtics as the "Hey, Bill" defense.

"Yes, 'Hey Bill,'" explained Bob Cousy. "You play your man tight, keep a hand in his face, stop his outside jumper. Then, if he beats you on the drive, you throw your hands up in the air and scream, 'Hey, Bill!' Then Russ picks him up and blocks the shot."

/ / /

Russell's influence did not end simply with the prevention of an opponent's scoring. Russell learned not only to knock down the opponents' shots, but also to bat them away in the direction of a teammate. The flow of the offensive team's players usually would be toward the basket for the shot or for rebounding as Russell knocked the ball the other way. As quick as Jones and other USF players were, they could grab the suddenly free ball as Russell batted it toward them and race downcourt for easy, fast break baskets. In the span of four or five seconds, the combination of a Russell block and then a Jones breakaway play might mean not only a four-point difference in the score, but also a jarring psychological impact. Russell not only defeated opponents, he emotionally shattered them.

The same quickness and leaping ability which made Russell a shot blocker made him an outstanding rebounder, too. As USF pressed defensively, keeping belly-to-belly with offensive men and forcing the flow of a game rather than simply reacting, opponents were forced to take poor percentage shots. When these shots bounced off the rim or off the backboard, Russell was usually there to retrieve the ball with well-timed leaps and then to permit USF to go to the offense.

It was a new kind of basketball in which, truly, USF's best offense was its Russell-inspired defense.

It took Russell his sophomore season to incorporate his skills into the team-wide style of play. There was maturity to be gained and there was further understanding to be exchanged between Russell and his coach. By the beginning of Russell's junior season, USF became literally as well as figuratively unbeatable, even though undercurrents of racial misunderstanding remained. Playing their home games at nearby Kezar Pavilion, an old municipally run facility, or at other temporary havens, USF won 55 consecutive games as well as two consecutive NCAA titles and was acclaimed the greatest college team of all time.

Russell astounded people. Still thinking in orthodox offensive basketball terms, they tended to deride his limited offensive repertoire and to question his aptitude for later professional stardom at the same time they praised him for his defense and rebounding.

In December 1955, USF walloped DePaul University of Chicago, 82-59. Bob Brachman, sportswriter for the San Francisco *Examiner,* asked the DePaul coach, Ray Meyer, to evaluate USF and to compare Russell with his one-time All-American star, George Mikan.

"I don't remember when I've ever seen a better college ball club," said the veteran coach. "We were never in the game!"

Meyer refused to concede Russell a personal edge over Mikan. "Russell is more agile and more mobile than Mikan as a college player and Russell is a better outside shot and a better defensive man," Meyer said. "Russell moves quickly and he doesn't foul. He picks up all shooters around the basket, which permits San Francisco to play an aggressive-type defense. He blocked ten shots in the first half and five in the second—all short shots—which against anyone else would have been sure baskets."

But Meyer showed his absorption in the pre-Russell basketball orthodoxy when he continued, "I think Mikan was easier to hit on the post. He backed his defensive man under the basket and always had such good position his teammates could pass to him. As a result, George had the ball sixty to seventy per cent of the time. In addition, Mikan was so big and strong that he carried his defensive man with him on the pivots. On rebounds, Russell tries to outjump and outreach his opponent. Mikan was an overpowering type of rebounder."

In San Francisco several days later, Brachman talked with Feerick about Meyer's evaluation of Russell and Mikan. Feerick had played against Mikan in the NBA and had coached against Russell . . . having failed, as he would admit 18 years later, to recruit him. "Of all the great things Russell does," Feerick told Brachman, "his rebounding is the greatest. He's the best rebounder I ever saw. He'd outjump Mikan by a good foot. It's tough to pick between the two, but, at the comparative stages of their careers, there's no question I'd have to take Russell because he's done a lot more for USF than Mikan did for DePaul."

/ / /

One man who could look past Russell's offensive deficiencies in the then-prevalent categories of shooting range and muscle power was a cigar-smoking, sometimes profane, always win-obsessed former Brooklyn, New York, schoolboy player named Arnold (Red) Auerbach. He coached the Boston Celtics, five-time NBA scoring leaders, but never champions despite their array of offensive stars including ball-handling wizard Bob Cousy and smooth-shooting Bill Sharman. In big games, the Celtics consistently were out-rebounded and therefore consistently lost.

Russell was picked for the United States Olympic Team which would play in Melbourne, Australia, in November 1956—already well into the pro season. The Rochester Royals had the poorest record in the league, and therefore the number-one draft pick, but needed more immediate help than Russell could provide by reporting to them as late as December. As a two-time All-American, he also would demand and deserve a bonus-salary agreement greater than the financially plagued Royals were interested in offering.

Second choice in the draft would go to Ben Kerner's struggling St. Louis Hawks. Kerner had operated as precariously as he could and still remain a franchise holder as he took the team from the "Tri-Cities" of Davenport, Iowa, Moline and Rock Island, Illinois, to Milwaukee in 1951. Wisconsin proved no haven, and Kerner had moved on to St. Louis in 1954. The Hawks had a fast-improving future star in 6-foot-9 Bob Pettit, former All-American at Lousiana State, but were still struggling to establish identity and popularity.

The city's most famous basketball product was lath-thin, sharp-shooting Ed Macauley . . . Easy Ed Macauley . . . who had been an All-American at St. Louis University immediately after the war. Macauley played with Boston, but, in 1956, was considering retirement to tend to business interests in his home city.

Auerbach, backed by the Celtics' owner, Walter Brown,

contacted the shrewd Kerner. NBA rules at the time forbade teams from trading their number-one draft choices, a restriction designed to force teams to try to improve themselves competitively rather than seek financial transfusions by giving up so valuable a commodity. But Auerbach and Kerner agreed that a deal sending Macauley (who would then continue his career) to St. Louis in exchange for the Hawks' top draft choice would help both teams. Kerner forced Auerbach to include rights to a 6-foot-4 former Kentucky All-American named Cliff Hagan, just returning to civilian life following a two-year Army hitch, and then the two pro basketball pioneers lobbied successfully among NBA owners for permission to complete the deal.

The Celtics honored Russell's amateurism by refraining from contacting him until after he had led the United States to the Olympic gold medal. The All-American returned to San Francisco early in December to wed his college sweetheart, the former Rose Swisher, and then reported, belatedly, to the Celtics.

Within his first four games with the Celtics, Russell established himself as a dominating new force in the sport. Although he was the only black on the Celtics and one of the few in the league at the time, he managed the difficult personal transition of moving to a strange new city and began to assert himself defensively and with his shot-blocking as startlingly as he had at USF. Rival coaches furiously claimed he was violating the NBA's rules against zone defenses by "playing a one-man zone" underneath rivals' baskets, swatting away what should have been easy layups or short-range jump shots. Auerbach merely grinned and urged the Celtics to play an even more aggressive style of defense than Russell's teammates had played at USF.

In college games, teams playing against Russell at least had the option of playing exaggeratedly slowed-down offenses. They could weave and move and pass from one man to another until, eventually, someone was free for a clear shot. The NBA's 24-second clock, introduced three seasons earlier, minimized the time an offense could work. The Celtics had only to apply pressure for 14 . . . 15 . . . 16 . . . seconds and the offenses began anxiously to look for a shot opportunity whether the range was too far or not, whether the shooter was off balance or not.

Should a man penetrate too close to the basket, having gotten around a pressing Celtic defender, he might find his shot smashed directly back at him or toward a sprinting Celtic by Russell's fast-reacting hands. Should a man shoot from too far away or without proper aim, the shot would miss and, then, another of Russell's greatnesses would manifest itself.

As a defensive rebounder, Russell had no peer. He had developed the stamina to leap again and again, never giving up on a rebound until it was clearly his or another man's. His timing was uncanny. He seemed to have a special intuition for where the ball might carom on a miss and a special ability to time his jump so that he was in position to pluck the ball away from other big men banging and slamming each other in that area around the backboards known affectionately as "The Butcher Shop."

Russell's defensive rebounds deprived opponents of second and third shot attempts, but, more vitally, permitted the Celtics to initiate the league's most effective fast break.

Russell often made his "outlet" pass, usually to Cousy, even before he returned to the floor after snaring the ball off the backboard or off the rim. Cousy, to permit this play, would move to the sideline—so Russell could spot him more quickly—as soon as an opponent shot. With the ball, Cousy could look first down floor for a teammate who might have broken free into scoring territory, or would begin dribbling down the middle of the court with one or more teammates flanking him, with a fourth just behind him and with Russell following—and sometimes overtaking—them. Two or more Celtics could converge on the basket against an outnumbered set of defenders for baskets achieved with devastating quickness. The contrast between the Celtics' quick scoring and a rival team's plodding efforts at maneuvering for a shot within the 24-second limit compounded Boston's psychological as well as tactical advantages.

/ / /

And, for 13 years, this pattern of play dominated pro basketball. Names changed and other teams sought pseudo-

Russells of their own, but it was Russell and the Celtics who dominated. The plodding NBA game of the Mikan era was extinct and the high-scoring, fast-action, fast-break, big-money game of today was born.

Said the volatile Auerbach after Russell led Boston to the 1956–57 championship with a title playoff victory over St. Louis, "Nothing Bill does surprises me any more. Without doubt, he's the greatest defensive player I have ever seen in my life, the greatest of all time. I'll go even further than that. He's twice as good as anybody else.

"His instincts, reflexes, and reactions are fabulous. He's got the perfect equipment—physical assets and desire. And what desire! He never stops running—and nobody, but nobody, can outrun that guy. Watch the way he gallops up and down the court. He's the first one to get to the baskets. And graceful? I've never seen such coordination in a big guy."

An ankle injury kept Russell out of the playoffs' deciding game in 1957–58 as St. Louis took the NBA title over Boston, but no team could match Russell or the Celtics in either regular season games or playoff pressure after that. Rather than being sated with one title after another, Russell and the Celtics hungered for even more victories, no matter the personal price to be paid. Russell never entered a significant game without being physically sick some time prior to opening tipoff. The sound of his retching and vomiting before a big game was as predictable and regular in the locker room as a growling admonition from Auerbach to keep up defensive pressure.

"Basketball," said Auerbach in 1963, "is like war in that offensive weapons are developed first, and it always takes a while for the defense to catch up. Russell has had the biggest impact on the game of anyone in the last ten years because he instituted a new defense weapon—that of the blocked shot. He has popularized the weapon to combat the aggressive, running-type game. He is by far the greatest center ever to play the game."

Russell, by now comfortable in his goatee, by now using his position as All-Pro athlete to speak out on social issues, by now confident of what he had done in basketball, explained exactly what his methods and efforts were. "Basketball is a game that involves a great deal of psychology," he said. "The psychology in defense is not blocking a shot or stealing a pass or getting the ball away. The psychology is to make the offensive team deviate from their normal habits. This is a game of habits, and the player with the most consistent habits is the best. What I try to do on defense is to make the offensive man do not what *he* wants, but what *I* want. I might block only five shots in a game . . . but I'm the only one who knows *which* five."

Basketball went well for Russell despite the intensity he could develop night after night, game after game to keep himself going. What was happening in America socially and his own position within the Boston area troubled him. He spoke out on the national issues first.

"The basic problem in Negro America," he said in 1963, "is the destruction of race pride. One could say we have been victims of psychological warfare, in a sense, in that this is a white country and all the emphasis is on being white. Whiter than white. According to the law, immigrants from northern European countries are more desirable than any others. When a white man says his folks come from Ireland, he says it with a certain amount of pride. He probably can trace his family tree for generations, for whatever it's worth. This is not true for the American Negro. Until the emergence of the independent African countries, all we knew about Africa was from Tarzan and Jungle Jim movies. How stupid they made the natives! One white man—Tarzan—was the best and smartest at everything. Pride in being black was practically destroyed. There was almost a sense of self-degradation.

"When I look at the struggle of the American Negro, I can't help but be very, very proud. With what we've had to work with, we've done a pretty good job of surviving. But we still have so far to go. . . ."

/ / /

In May 1973, Russell returned to the NBA by accepting the dual roles of coach and general manager of the Seattle Sonics. It was 10 years after his dramatic pronouncements about the role of the Negro in America. He had been among the first Negro personalities to speak out on such issues at the risk of alienating white fans and the white establishment. His concern

Triumphant once again, Bill Russell laughs his cackle laugh, running off The Forum court in Los Angeles after his final championship and final game as leader of the Boston Celtics

for a lack of pride among Negroes had been expressed later and eloquently as Black Pride and Black Power. The very terms were different now—no longer capital N *Negro,* but small b *black.* But Russell was no less outspoken. He told Seattle writers about inequities and indignities he had suffered in Boston and in the suburb of Reading, where he and his family had lived.

"What I said in Seattle last summer was that the years in Boston were very traumatic," Russell explained. "I didn't enjoy my stay there. I didn't live in a vacuum. I'm talking about Roxbury [Boston's black ghetto community], but also about my own experience and about Reading. I couldn't stay on the court all my life. That's only forty-eight minutes out of the day. That's what I mean about not living in a vacuum."

The horizons of pro basketball had been too confining, finally, he admitted. Even the challenges of coaching, he'd found, could not keep his attitude toward basketball fresh. He had retired and sought a new life style, new vistas. While his wife and three children remained in Massachussetts (there later was a divorce), Russell moved to Hollywood at the urging of a good friend, pro football superstar-turned-film-star Jim Brown, to seek a new career in show business.

Although much in demand and popular as a lecturer at colleges throughout the country, Russell found that roles were limited for 6-foot-9¾ romantic leads or even for 6-foot-9¾ character actors. In several acting roles and in appearances on comedy-variety television shows, Russell displayed a pointed wit and special charm that led to a well-rated nightly phone-in radio talk show—on sports and social issues generally—in Los Angeles and a job bringing him back to the NBA at least once each week. Russell became "color man" on NBA Game of the Week broadcasts for the American Broadcasting Co. In this role, Russell's candor and cackling laughter made him nationally popular all over again, albeit in a new way. He was the most truthful, least sponsor-serving, least cliché-spouting commentator in big-time network sports.

"Have you ever seen a game as hard-fought, as emotion-filled as this one?" a near-hysterical broadcasting partner asked Russell once.

"Yes," said Russell calmly. And he left it at that.

During a New York Knicks broadcast once, the cameras focused on an unlikely personage who called himself "Dancing Harry." A black from Baltimore, he had attached himself to Earl (The Pearl) Monroe as a special sort of one-man fan club. "Dancing Harry" pranced and danced and made voodoo gestures at rival teams at Madison Square Garden. He was tolerated with amusement by players and Knicks' officials. Russell observed Dancing Harry's gyrations this time, Eddie Layton's organ music blaring syncopated accompaniment to the high-stepping weirdness. "Hmm," mused Russell. "Contrary to popular belief, obviously we ain't *all* got rhythm."

/ / /

Russell was the player who taught a young sportswriter named Harris how, above all, the mental and emotional may transcend—in rare men—mere physical skill in sport. Russell showed how a man may *will* himself to achievement even if his body balks at being punished further. He taught me, just by his example, as I watched him in title series after title series against the Lakers and other teams, that manhood in sport may be demonstrated by higher values than bulging muscles and hairy chests.

Researching this book and reviewing millions of words by Russell and his peers, I found a speech by this unique, pattern-setting individual which seems best to sum up his special personal distinction and style. He praised Cousy, but in his eloquence more truly honored himself.

He spoke in Boston in April 1963, the night after the Celtics had defeated Los Angeles for what was their fifth consecutive world championship. Cousy retired from the NBA with that victory, and the traditional Celtic "break up" dinner was held, as the team disbanded until the following fall, in his honor.

"I do not consider myself a real good basketball player," Russell said. "I consider myself a *great* basketball player. Egotism is as important in the game as ability.

"In the seven years I've played with Bob Cousy, I've always respected him as a player. Professional jealousy does exist. But I can honestly say I've never resented Cooz.

"In basketball, we're all good. Forget that. We're like a

family. We see each other on this team as brothers, not as athletes. This man, just by being himself, has meant so much to all of us. What Cousy did you can never find words for.

"This is a foolish game we play. Grown men playing kid games.

"Championships are nice, wonderful. Take seven titles and you still need a dime for a cup of coffee. These are superficial things.

"The friendships are what are lasting. The friendship of this man is something that can never die."

3

GOLIATH IN A MULTI-MILLION-DOLLAR MANSION: WILT CHAMBERLAIN

Two floors below street level in the yellow and orange pseudo-Greek monument of impressario Jack Kent Cooke's Forum in the Los Angeles suburb of Inglewood, California, cold and bare concrete corridors connect the dressing rooms of the athletes and show-business stars who entertain masses of Southern Californians there on more than 250 nights each year.

In May 1973 a bearded black man, nearly seven feet tall and wearing a gold blazer with an American Broadcasting Company crest on its breast pocket, walked briskly on his spidery legs toward the entrance to the New York Knicks' dressing room. Shouts of congratulations and joy leaked through the heavy wooden door to mark what should have been an entirely joyous occasion.

As Bill Russell reached for the handle so that he could enter, grab a microphone, and begin interviews with members of the newly crowned world champions, the door opened.

Dipping his head to clear the doorway in a gesture which, long ago, had given him a favored nickname—the Big Dipper—Wilt Chamberlain emerged. In his hand he carried a mangled and still-wet terry-cloth headband. On his wrists were two smaller, drenched sweatbands, also purple and gold-colored to coordinate with his uniform. Perspiration flowed in miniature rivers down his high brow and dripped in great drops from his beard onto his warmup jacket.

His head was down. He had just performed the unhappy, but sporting, gesture of entering his vanquishers' dressing quarters even before returning to his own. He'd congratu-lated the Knicks for the victory, recognizing that the game ended his and his team's one-year reign as kings of the NBA.

As Chamberlain stepped through the doorway, his immense frame emerging from the room the way a dozen circus clowns emerge from a trick mini-mobile, he saw Russell walking toward him. In that same moment, Russell looked up and saw Chamberlain.

They were within an arm's length of each other at that moment, two giants who had played scores of basketball games against each other, two men compared endlessly and pointlessly with each other, two men whose careers and lives are perpetually intertwined.

There was a split second of flinty, awkward recognition. Two sets of hard, restless eyes made contact as brief as the electronic interconnection between computer components. Then, in incredible and jarring disregard for each other, the men walked onward toward their destinations, attempting to pretend to each other and themselves that the other did not exist. It was cold. Icy cold. And to a sportswriter who hap-pened to see it, it was terribly, terribly sad.

/ / /

Once, they had been friends. They were, after all, co-members of one of mankind's most select and put-upon fra-ternities—gianthood—and they had talked of their unique problems and unique basketball roles often and warmly ear-lier in their lives.

Russell, 3 inches shorter and at least 35 or more pounds lighter than Chamberlain, was the defensive genius. Chamberlain was, for much of his career, the offensive juggernaut: the one the immoveable object, the other the ir-resistible force—the classic confrontation. Their battles through 10 seasons of NBA combat were epic. They were ultimate savor for the fans of that special *one-on-one* matchup of superstars which distinguishes pro basketball from other games.

Usually in their regular season and playoff battles, Chamberlain had emerged with superior individual statistics and Russell with a team victory. Usually, Chamberlain would be forced to explain afterward he didn't care for personal congratulations paid him for his own achievements because his team had lost. Usually, Russell would cackle thankfully that his team had won even though he, personally, might have been outrebounded or outscored. Tacit in their relationship was the mutual knowledge each was doing in games what helped best their respective sets of teammates . . . and that, more often than not, it was Russell who played with the more talented group.

The incident which opened the final breach between the two great hero figures was, fittingly, national in scope, oft-betold, fascinatingly revealing of major personality traits of the two protagonists . . . and trivial.

In April 1969, Russell climaxed his incredible career by leading Boston to a come-from-behind, upset, final-championship-game victory over a dissension-plagued Laker team at the Forum. It was the second straight title for player-coach Russell and his eleventh in thirteen seasons. Chamberlain had come to the Lakers in a trade during the summer of 1968, joining superstars Jerry West and Elgin Baylor in what was expected to have been the strongest lineup of all time. Instead, Chamberlain was ill used by Coach Butch van Breda Kolff and feuded vigorously with him all season in arguments which nearly tore the team apart.

The Lakers managed to reach the NBA title series despite all the turmoil and were favored, with the seventh-game home-court advantage because of a better regular-season record than Boston, to defeat the Celtics for the first time in a championship showdown.

West entered the final game at less than 30 per cent of his usual capability, limping painfully because of a torn thigh muscle, and late in the fourth period, Chamberlain began limping, too. A knee had plagued him all season. A rebounding battle ensued from which Wilt emerged with the ball, but

Powerfully awesome in mid-career, Wilt Chamberlain bombards basket for his Dipper Dunk . . . basketball's all-time most devastating play

from which he landed awkwardly. The game had to be stopped momentarily and Wilt, the bad knee throbbing agonizingly, had to be helped to the sidelines.

Shortly afterward, the Lakers attempting desperately to rally, Wilt notified van Breda Kolff that he could return to combat, that the pain had ebbed. Van Breda Kolff ignored Wilt, and the Lakers wound up losing . . . as they probably would have to the inspired Celtics in any case.

It was the game, basketball fans will recall, for which Jack Kent Cooke had ordered hundreds of balloons inflated and kept aloft in the upper reaches of the Forum in huge nets. He had hired the University of Southern California marching band. He'd anticipated a rain of multi-colored balloons and the brass playing of "Happy Days Are Here Again" as celebration of a Laker championship. Instead, when Russell and the Celtics won, the balloons stayed up and the band went quietly back to its campus.

Russell had not announced publicly he had decided to retire with that last game. Chamberlain, in a comparable situation, would have mentioned to some of his friends in the media the news he was considering retirement. Russell does things secretly, deciding issues by himself; Chamberlain tends to think out loud and, sometimes, without discretion.

Looking for a career in show business and not planning to confirm his retirement from the Celtics until the fall, Russell accepted a series of college lecture dates including one, in May, at the University of Wisconsin. Outspoken and honest to a fault, Russell was asked that day what his reaction had been to Chamberlain's alleged failure to lead the Lakers to the championship and about Wilt's absence from the lineup during the title game's climactic moments. Russell refrained from the mutually protective pap which athletes ordinarily use in deference to each other's sensitivities. He gave a truthful reply.

He was not aware that a reporter for a local newspaper was in the audience, nor could he anticipate that his comments would become national headlines within the next few hours.

"Any injury short of a broken leg or a broken back isn't good enough," Russell charged. "When Wilt took himself out of the final game, when he hurt his knee—well, I wouldn't have put him back in the game, either."

The reporter scribbled notes furiously as Russell, his goatee bobbing, continued. "I never said Chamberlain didn't have talent. But basketball is a team game. I go by the number of championships. I play to bring out the best in my teammates. Are you going to say that he brought out the best in Elgin and Jerry?

"I'd have to say yes and no as to whether criticism about Wilt is justified. No, because people see his potential as greater than it is. They don't take human frailties into consideration. Yes, because he asks for it. He talks a lot about what he's going to do. What it's all about is winning and losing, and he's done a lot of losing. He thinks he's a genius. He isn't."

The circumstances of Russell's comments—that they were solicited rather than volunteered and that they'd been expressed at a convocation of college students rather than to a group of sportswriters—weren't reported. The lashing bitterness *was* reported . . . and then repeated and re-repeated. Newspaper librarians across the nation faithfully filed clippings of the Wisconsin speech story and sportswriters seemed to find them often when they sought background material through which to express anger at the latest real or alleged Chamberlain transgression.

Chamberlain saw the original story the day after Russell's shockingly severe rebuke. Accused of feigning an injury to avoid playing—and possibly failing—in a crucial situation, Chamberlain was still tender-kneed and had, in fact, canceled what would have been a lucrative tour of Europe with the Harlem Globetrotters.

Proud and sensitive, he was hurt that Russell had so publicly and, in his view, unfairly criticised him. Henceforth, as Russell moved to Los Angeles and became both a nightly talk-show host and national television commentator there, Chamberlain considered him an enemy. They were in the same arenas often, but never resumed their original closeness . . . or even mutual respect.

Frequently on his talk show, Russell was asked by young listeners, innocently, why he never interviewed Chamberlain on his show or during halftimes of NBA Games of the Week. "It's hard to interview someone," Russell would respond, his voice breaking into that cackle of a laugh, "when you're not talking to him."

/ / /

Because Russell had been on the air, wise, smiling . . . and cackling that laugh of his . . . his national image remained that of all-winning hero even when his Seattle Sonics failed at first to live up to the high expectations expressed when Russell became their coach.

Chamberlain was the villain to begin with, and his image suffered another major jolt in the fall of 1973 when he jumped from the Los Angeles Lakers and the NBA to the San Diego Conquistadors of the ABA.

Chamberlain was to earn a reported $600,000 as player-coach of the San Diego team. The owner, Dr. Leonard Bloom, was a 38-year-old orthodontist with a flair for investments and fund-raising. He hoped to parlay Wilt's appearances into voters' approval in a special referendum in the San Diego suburb of Chula Vista for a $20 million arena-shopping center.

The plan and the team soured when Wilt was restricted solely to a coaching role because of the demands of the option clause in his NBA contract, upheld by the courts in a suit brought by the Lakers. The plan collapsed altogether when the people of Chula Vista refused to sanction the building of the huge complex on grounds of adverse ecological and social impact.

The Conquistadors, an expansion franchise formed only a year before, won more games than they had a right to under Chamberlain's coaching, but Wilt continued to treasure his privacy. He accepted few appointments arranged for interviews with San Diego area news media, and some which he accepted he canceled abruptly. A coach in pro basketball must be readily accessible, and this was a condition Wilt seldom has been willing to grant.

Rather than become a resident of San Diego, Wilt continued to live in Los Angeles . . . in the $1.5 million pleasure dome of a bachelor mansion which he named Ursa Major . . . or to translate from the Latin of astronomers, the Big Dipper—i.e., Wilt himself. All triangular shapes, massive in scope and furnishings, bright with colors, the home sprawls over three acres of an expensive mountaintop site high in the Santa Monica Mountains, overlooking the luxury of Beverly Hills and the Pacific Ocean to one side and the housing-development sprawl of the San Fernando Valley to the other. Much was made of the home as Wilt built it and moved into it, and its sensational, sensual features did not endear him to people living in humdrum, orthodox $30,000 split-levels.

Finally, Chamberlain published a ghost-written autobiography in 1973 which, if anything, was far less revealing of the inner Chamberlain than it might have been. Instead of balancing some lurid tales of Wilt's romantic escapades against details of his work with Richard M. Nixon and other national figures, the autobiography perpetuated Chamberlain's image as a self-centered boor. Rather than express Chamberlain's social views and the depth of his knowledge of basketball dynamics, the autobiography criticised many people in the sport.

At a time when Chamberlain was to have reported to training with the Lakers and to have attempted to resolve contract
differences with the team, he was on a personal-appearances
tour promoting the book. He confirmed reports of his choice
of San Diego over Los Angeles while on tour, too.

Thus, as he had done so often in his career, Chamberlain
was doing the unpopular thing in an unpopular way, permitting a logical and defendable career step to be cast in the worst
possible light.

/ / /

Some things Chamberlain cannot evade. He is black. He is
huge. He is a great athletic star. He is perpetually on public
display any time he emerges from his mansion. As often as he
is able, he eats in his hotel rooms or at his home; he cannot sit
down at a restaurant table without attracting stares and
crowds of autograph-seekers.

A lifetime of this sort of thing has produced a personality
that is all paradox and enigma. The personality is quicksil-
ver—impossible to define because his moods change endlessly
and restlessly as he moves, a giant, through a world made for
smaller men. In a reflection on himself which has followed
him as both a defiant banner and sad epithet, he noted bitterly
once, "Nobody roots for Goliath." Beyond all other giants who
have been in public focus, he epitomizes that truth about
man's intolerance for superman.

His career has been so charged with controversy and his
accomplishments in athletics and business so monumental that
he has been, more truly than any other basketball player, an
international celebrity. A definition of this term is that no
description and no details are required for instant and univer-
sal recognition other than the utterance of a name. There is
only one Elvis . . . there is only one Liz . . . there is only one
Frank . . . there was only one Marilyn . . . and there is only one
Wilt.

His life has had a seasonal pattern from his beginnings as
one of nine children born to the family of a custodian for the
Curtis Publishing Company in Philadelphia through his late
career as a star of the Los Angeles Lakers. Already 6-foot-10
by the time he was 15 years old, Chamberlain has been a

dynamic and significant competitive figure during each basketball season, a controversial and news-making figure each off-season.

In a burst of special generosity, members of the National Basketball Association Board of Governors accorded draft rights to him to owner Eddie Gottlieb of the Philadelphia Warriors even before the boy left Overbrook High School as, already, a nationally known figure.

After two seasons on the University of Kansas varsity, he left college to criticize the stall tactics and trick defenses used against him and joined the international clowning of the Globetrotters for a year.

After his rookie season as a pro, he announced in a national magazine story he would retire.

Another year, he permitted a national magazine to headline an article ghost-written for him, "My Life in a Bush League," earning a rebuke and a fine from the NBA's commissioner.

Some summers, he was going to jump teams or jump leagues.

Two different summers, he was going to turn prizefighter for a challenge of heavyweight champion Muhammad Ali in a bout which would overwhelmingly have been the most lucrative of all time; Ali and his advisors reneged on their agreement, but Wilt was eager to see it through.

Another summer, 1968, he refused the chance to become player-coach of the Philadelphia 76ers and, instead, engineered a trade which permitted him to play in his adopted home city, Los Angeles.

Whatever the controversy of a given year, the flurry of July and August was usually debunked and forgotten by November and the next season. But Chamberlain's national image as temperamental and conniving grew with each incident.

When Joe Mullaney of Providence College was named to replace van Breda Kolff as the coach of the Lakers in 1969, virtually the only question asked of him at a sumptuous press conference staged by Jack Kent Cooke was, "How will you handle Wilt Chamberlain?" Mullaney gave polite, correctly vague, correctly optimistic answers.

Chamberlain was a special celebrity guest later that week at the opening of a lush new Las Vegas hotel. Reporters sought him out for comments about the new coach and about that coach's comments about him.

"*Animals* are 'handled,' not men," Wilt responded bristlingly. "I'll do my job."

To those who had decided that Chamberlain was a self-serving, egotistical boor, the comment seemed a snarl of defiance, perfectly in character for an athlete who allegedly refused to be coached and who supposedly refused to become truly part of any team.

To the minority who held affection for him, that first public statement about a new coach could be interpreted as a realistic—incisive, in fact—assertion of a man's self-image. It was a demonstration of another facet of his personality—pride.

/ / /

That he is physically mightier than all but a few men has not made him less sensitive to insult or pain. A lifetime of being regarded as a freak and of being constantly on public display has left him vulnerable to critics, try as he may to feign lack of interest. Often, he has read insult into comments which may have been unfeeling, but which were not as pointedly critical of him as he interpreted them to be.

An example of this supersensitivity to real or alleged insult came in January of 1970, when Wilt was in the midst of the strenuous rehabilitation which followed the knee-tendon surgery which had sidelined him two months before. The NBA All-Star Game was to take place in Philadelphia that year, and Philadelphia was his native city. Nine straight years he had been virtually an automatic choice to the All-Star Game roster, but his first serious athletic injury had denied him the honor a tenth time and he was hurt that he had not been given some sort of special recognition, considering the game was to be played in his original home town.

"It wouldn't be precedent," he said moodily. "I know at other All-Star Games they've been hospitable to old stars from the past. I think I'm due as much. I know for a fact that an official of the Lakers suggested it. Nothing doing. So I'll come to Philadelphia to visit my mother and buy my own ticket."

Wilt did just that, and the dramatic entrance he made at the

Spectrum sidelines just before the opening tipoff that night became another chapter in his legend. He strode into the building with a slight limp, wearing a crushed velvet, plum-colored shirt over matching pants and accented by the huge gold Egyptian *ankh* dangling from his neck on a heavy gold chain. ("A girl gave it to me—a girl I met in Europe," he explained.)

He walked tall and proud, yet without special care to call attention to himself, and, as he approached the sidelines to offer handshakes of best wishes to a few of his fellow pros, Chamberlain suddenly was the focus of attention for everyone in the building. Just by being there, he turned an oversight by the league into a personal triumph.

Willis Reed of the Knicks was the Most Valuable Player, but Wilt was the topic of conversation in the corridors beneath the stands and later at the postgame party. He had made his point.

His sensitivity was demonstrated again in 1971 shortly after Joe Mullaney was discharged as coach of the Lakers and Bill Sharman was named to succeed him.

Those close to the club were aware that Mullaney's ouster had been a necessary, though difficult, decision. An even-tempered, likable guy, devoted to his family, an authority on theories and execution of defensive basketball, Mullaney had established too loose a discipline for so ego-involved a team as the Lakers. Sharman, who had guided Utah to the American Basketball Association championship and who is noted in basketball for demanding intensity and concentration from his players, was an ideal choice.

Yet, in the confusion surrounding the change, many in Southern California assumed—out of habit as much as anything—that Mullaney had been made expendable because of friction with Wilt.

"Why does the public and press always blame me?" Wilt asked plaintively. "I believe the owner has the right to fire anyone he wants to. I got along fine with Joe. Before him, van Breda Kolff was a slightly different thing. Sure, I had confrontations with Butch, but Mr. Cooke didn't think he was doing a good job, so he was fired. It's the nature of the sport.

"I always am used as a scapegoat. Mr. Cooke is a very strong and outspoken man, but he does nothing to protect me from these charges. As to the new coach, I'm not going to worry about Sharman. I like the idea of being an individual, but I do the best I can in team play."

For once, Wilt proved an accurate prophet. Sharman brought to the Lakers a knack for organization and preparation they'd not known since 1967, when Fred Schaus stepped upward from coach to general manager. Instead of telling the Lakers how old they were and accepting sluggish play because of alleged athletic senility, Sharman had the Lakers accelerate. "I think it's a lot less wearing on a team to get a quick, fast-break basket," the new coach said, "than it is to come down and grind it out." And the Lakers saw this was true.

A quick, smart young forward from Columbia University, Jim McMillian, proved so adept at the running game he could not be kept out of the starting lineup. Superstar Elgin Baylor chose to retire rather than fall to the status of McMillian's reserve. McMillian and guard Gail Goodrich were urged to break for their goal as soon as an opponent attempted a shot. Chamberlain consistently gathered the defensive rebound and fired long passes to the two quick, relatively small men for breakaway, uncontested layups. Jerry West was freed, for the first time in his career, from the pressure of having to emphasize his scoring. Instead, he could roam, be a playmaker, and spearhead a pressing, gambling defense keyed to the awesome presence of Chamberlain underneath the basket.

The Lakers went through the entire month of November undefeated. Christmas passed and the Lakers still had not lost. Not until January 9, 1972, after 33 consecutive wins, were the Lakers defeated—by Milwaukee at Milwaukee. Their subsequent world championship-series victory over the New York Knicks was a joyous vindication for Sharman, Chamberlain, the players, and the management: for at least one year, they were supreme in all of basketball.

Wilt played the deciding seventh game of the championship series with a hairline fracture in his right hand and with a sprained left hand, protected by a pair of the huge pads worn by defensive linemen in football. It was a demonstration of selflessness and willingness to absorb pain that directly refuted

Turning his power to defense and rebounding, Wilt Chamberlain soars high above New York's Willis Reed to retrieve an errant field-goal attempt on behalf of Los Angeles Lakers

the biting criticism by Russell which had ended their friend-ship. The championship dispelled . . . for at least a summer . . . Chamberlain's image as a loser.

Wilt himself was one of the first to point out a great irony. In his high-school, collegiate, and early professional career, he played a power game emphasizing—because his coaches and pro executive bosses wanted him to—his ability to score points seemingly at will. Those teams had not won championships. With the Lakers, coached by a former Boston Celtic, Cham-berlain became the defensive focus whose shot-blocking and defensive rebounding initiated the Lakers' most effective offense. He was playing, in fact, *Bill Russell basketball.* And it won a world championship.

Had Sharman created, as he was credited with doing, a "new Chamberlain?" Wilt denied it and Sharman denied it. Instead there had been quick and easy agreement between the two veterans that, given the Lakers' personnel and needs, this was the best way for him to play.

Sharman's arrival as Laker coach brought the same volley of questions about his intentions toward the superstar as had greeted van Breda Kolff when Wilt was traded to the Lakers and Mullaney when he replaced van Breda Kolff. As had his two predecessors, Sharman gave cautiously diplomatic answers.

Privately, Sharman was concerned. He'd tried unsuccess-fully to reach Chamberlain by phone in order to arrange a meeting with him as he had with other Lakers shortly after being hired. Chamberlain hadn't returned Sharman's calls and, as the opening of preseason camp began, the new coach worried.

"It's gotta be something personal and special," Sharman was assured by a mutual friend. "Wilt wants to play for a good basketball team and what you want is a good basketball team. There's no reason to anticipate any problems."

Twenty-four hours later, Chamberlain still had not returned Sharman's calls . . . but he did return a call from that mutual friend. "I'm going through a sort of negotiation thing with Jack Kent Cooke," Wilt said. "It's nothing against Bill, it's just that my attorneys and I feel I shouldn't have anything to do with the team until we get my contract settled."

Having manifested with this ploy some of his keen business sense, Chamberlain did reach agreement with Cooke within the next several days. He then became one of the hardest workers when Sharman finally gathered his players to prepare for the season.

The first two weeks were spent on conditioning drills and unstructured scrimmaging merely to get the feel of things after a summer's idleness. Then, at a workout at Iolani High School gym in Honolulu, where the Lakers were to play the Milwaukee Bucks and Phoenix Suns in a pair of exhibition games, Sharman sort of casually strolled over to Chamberlain on the sidelines during a pause in scrimmage, as though he had nothing more complicated in mind than a chat about the weather.

"You know," said Sharman, "I'd like to get your ideas on how you think you'd like to play . . . some of your thinking about the game. For instance, with the Celts, we used to funnel everything on defense into Russ. . . ."

Chamberlain nodded assent, and, in what Sharman carefully had staged as apparently a casual gesture, the two men began earnestly to discuss what grew to be the Lakers' world-championship pattern. There had been truly an exchange of ideas, for Sharman recognized still another truism about Chamberlain that has usually gone unrecognized—that he has played under some of the game's greatest coaches and that he has, in time, developed a keen insight into the game.

/ / /

The "new Chamberlain" was the evolved product of 13 seasons in the NBA beginning in 1959, when he became the first man ever to be selected the league's Rookie of the Year and Most Valuable Player simultaneously.

The Chamberlain of that season had not reached full physical maturity, but already was stronger physically than any other player in the league. Encouraged to score points because of scoring's box-office lure and because the Warriors were not an especially talented team otherwise, Chamberlain averaged 37.6 points per game, taking an average of nearly 35 field-goal attempts each night. His playing style was as unorthodox as his success was unique.

Where George Mikan and most outstanding centers after

him developed a power hook shot which drew them toward the basket to follow their shots and capitalize on their muscle, Chamberlain's pet play was his "fadeaway jump shot" launched from the left side of the key and from 10 to 12 feet out. He would get down in *low post* position near the basket in the way Mikan and others had always done, wait for someone to pass the ball in to him, and then take a step out and *away* from the basket as he twisted in mid-air and bulleted his shot in what was actually a downward trajectory.

There was no possible way for an opponent to block the shot, so high was Wilt's leap and so forceful was his shot. But the momentum of his body carried him away from, rather than toward, the basket, and on the shots which missed he'd be too far out of the play, usually, to rebound well. Rivals quickly grasped this flaw in his game and began bullying him and pressuring him further and further away from the basket. The shot couldn't be blocked, but at least his percentage could be reduced, and a miss gave an opponent a good chance at the defensive rebound.

He averaged 46.1 per cent field-goal accuracy as a rookie, improving to 50.9 per cent and 38.4 points per game the next season.

In his third year as a pro, still relying heavily on his fadeaway jumper, but at full strength and maturity so that few men were able to shove him out of his chosen position, Chamberlain accomplished the incredible by *averaging* 50.4 points per game for a full season. He capped it all on March 20, 1962, when he scored 100 points in a 169-147 victory over the New York Knicks at Hershey, Pennsylvania.

All the while, Russell was averaging less than 20 points per game, winning world championships . . . and earning acclaim as Chamberlain's superior.

In 1962, rotund and wise Eddie Gottlieb, a founding father of pro basketball, decided to move the franchise from Philadelphia to San Francisco in an attempt to mine the same kind of gold Minneapolis businessman Bob Short had found two years earlier when he moved his Laker franchise to Los Angeles. The first season of transition was personally and competitively difficult for the team, but Chamberlain adapted quickly to the cosmopolitan city and continued his personal assault on the record books with a scoring average of 44.8.

The free-throw lane had been widened from 12 to its present 16 feet across in a rule change admittedly instigated—unsuccessfully—as a means of diminishing Chamberlain's domination of the game.

Resourceful Alex Hannum, a one-time journeyman pro whose special coaching assets were contagious intensity and a muscular 6-foot-7 frame which outsized and intimidated most of his players, became the Warriors' coach for their second season in the West.

Gottlieb had insisted the Warriors not pass up the opportunity to draft Nate Thurmond, a 6-foot-11 youngster from Bowling Green, Ohio, even though in Chamberlain the Warriors were blessed already with the strongest and most durable center in the game. Hannum used the rookie as a forward along with a 6-foot-6 ex-San Francisco youngster named Tom Meschery to go with a backcourt including clever Guy Rodgers and a poor-shooting, strong defense-playing second-year man from New Jersey named Al Attles.

It wasn't a quick team at all. Instead, the Warriors utilized what Hannum loudly and frequently proclaimed as "muscle and hustle," and the club outfinished Los Angeles to win the Western Division championship. Boston won the East, of course, and it was all but inevitable that the Celtics and Russell should capture the over-all league title in their championship-series confrontation.

The most significant aspect of the season was that Chamberlain's scoring average dipped from the 44.8 points per game of 1962–63 to 36.9. He took fewer shots than ever before in his career, restricting in particular the fadeaway jumpers which opponents had all but urged him to attempt in the preceding seasons as their best hope of minimizing his impact.

The Warriors' pace was plodding. Chamberlain, often having plucked off the defensive rebound, would lope down court. Rodgers was the playmaker, and he would pass in to Wilt as soon as the bigger man stationed himself in his favorite position, deep and to the left of the basket.

The great change was that, instead of wheeling for his

fadeaway jumper most of the time as he had done before, Chamberlain more often stood his ground. He'd hold the ball aloft, often in just one huge hand, and then swoop with strength and monstrous stride toward the basket for his other patented play, the spectacularly forceful Dipper Dunk which propelled the ball directly through the basket at point-blank range. An alternative was for Chamberlain to pass to a team-mate freed for an open shot as opponents sagged back on Wilt in an attempt to prevent his dunk.

This, and not the pattern of the Sharman regime in Los Angeles eight years later, was the *new Chamberlain.* He was almost always in good offensive rebounding position by vir-tually ignoring his fadeaway jumper. His passing from the pivot made his teammates much better scoring threats than they might possibly have been free-lancing or working one-on-one by themselves. Later, in Los Angeles, Sharman's suc-cess came not from teaching Wilt to mesh with his teammates, but rather by teaching the Lakers to mesh with Wilt.

Chamberlain's off-season newsmaking in the summer of 1964 was medical rather than controversial. He developed an agonizing burning sensation in his stomach that left him weak and sleepless. San Francisco doctors were unable to help him as preseason camp began without him. He returned to Phila-delphia, where Dr. Stan Lorber of the Temple University Medical Center discovered he had developed an inflamma-tion of the pancreas. A special diet was prescribed which there-after restricted the kinds of foods he could eat . . . fortunately not restricting volume, which was then and remains now appropriately gigantic.

By the time he reported to the Warriors, the team was floundering both artistically and at the gate. Rumors of a trade for him or for young Thurmond abounded. The Lakers had a chance to get him, but the issue was put to a vote of players and the tally was negative. Finally, late on the night of the mid-season All-Star Game in St. Louis, Chamberlain was traded to the Philadelphia 76ers, the former Syracuse fran-chise which had been shifted to Philadelphia following the Warriors' departure. It has never been denied that an aspect of the trade was that it permitted the Warriors to get off the hook for Chamberlain's salary, which already had soared beyond $100,000.

It took Chamberlain and the 76ers the remainder of the season and all of 1965–66 to mesh completely. Former All-Pro Dolph Schayes was the coach, but he was an easygoing personality who failed to provide strong direction for a team of young veterans. In 1966–67, Schayes was replaced by Hannum, who, earlier in the off-season, had been fired by new owner Franklin Mieuli of San Francisco.

The reunion of Chamberlain and Hannum, the maturity of several young players, and the addition of a quick 6-foot-6 rookie forward named Billy Cunningham culminated in what many observers—including the author—consider to have been, for its one season, the finest team in basketball history.

Chamberlain was indomitable at center, a defensive obstacle every bit as efficient as Russell and able to score almost any time he wanted to, it seemed, on offense. Smooth 6-foot-6 Chet Walker provided firepower and mobility at one forward position and 6-foot-9 Lucious Jackson complemented Chamberlain beautifully on the boards at the other. Heady and steady Hal Greer was a brilliant mid-range jump-shooter at one guard and Wally Jones was a firebrand playmaker at the other. And with Cunningham, Larry Costello, Dave Gambee, Bill Melchionni, and rookie Matty Goukas, there was plenty of bench strength, too.

Chamberlain averaged only 24.1 points per game, just third best in the league, as the 76ers ravaged their foes for 68 victories in 81 games, a pro record which stood until the Lakers went 69-13 in a 1971–72 league weakened by multiple expansions.

These were good days for Wilt. He lived in a plush apartment on Central Park in New York, commuting to Philadelphia for games. His business investments flourished. His health was good. He seemed to make *not* scoring almost as much a point of pride as scoring had been before. He screened for teammates and he averaged nearly eight assists per game, third in the league only to Oscar Robertson and Guy Rodgers, and went an entire game once without attempting a shot.

When he felt the 76ers needed offense, however, he could turn on the power as effectively as ever. A 43-point outburst against Baltimore on February 11 and 58 against Cincinnati two nights later silenced sceptical Philadelphians who said Wilt's reduced scoring meant he was slowing with age.

It took this machine just four games to dispose of Cincinnati and only five to dethrone Boston for victory in the Eastern Division playoffs. When San Francisco carried the 76ers to as many as six games in the world championship playoffs, it was considered a moral victory for the West Coast team. No one called Chamberlain a loser that summer.

The next season brought 62 wins on the court, but problems developed within the 76er franchise which led to an upset loss to regular-season runner-up Boston in the Eastern Division playoffs. Hannum resigned as coach, Chamberlain declined the post, and, in July, he dealt personally with Jack Kent Cooke to complete the trade which sent him to Los Angeles.

Controversy followed him. He feuded with van Breda Kolff. He was injured under Mullaney. He won a world championship with Sharman. He feuded with Cooke over contract terms. After taking the Lakers to the final playoff series once again, he turned to San Diego and the ABA. And, finally, in the fall of 1974, he left pro basketball to pursue new interests and new pleasures. Finally, he was free of daily scrutiny.

But, in the meantime, he remained the most respected player in the league for his strength and for his ability to take sheer physical command of key games.

/ / /

In his playing style, Chamberlain was an individualist, but not—as was Russell—an innovator. His great contribution to his fellow pros was his successful bargaining for greater and greater rewards. When he reached $100,000 for the first time, the Celtics responded by paying Russell $100,001. The pay scale around the NBA rose proportionately. Today, basketball players average more money per season than any other set of professional athletes.

His goatee and his fondness for flamboyant, self-designed clothing helped establish a life style shared now by the

Andy Witherspoon, Long Beach News Bureau

There's no national attention or big-time pressure in off season as Wilt Chamberlain strides into a serve for his "Wilt's Big Dippers" exhibition volleyball team

majority of athletes. He did not publicly protest injustices to blacks, but he contributed privately to important civil-rights projects and, at the funeral of the Reverend Dr. Martin Luther King in 1968, he marched in the front rank.

His friends come from the ghetto and from the swankiest circles of Beverly Hills and Hollywood society. On his arm and, presumably, in his boudoir, have appeared parades of beautiful women of a variety of ages and races. Witty, wealthy, entertaining, and considerate of his friends and house guests, Chamberlain at his most charming is a warm host.

Is it surprising that the attention of such a charismatic man should melt as many feminine hearts as he claims in his memoirs? Hardly, and for more reasons than merely the *machismo* his lurid autobiography suggests.

During his convalescence from knee surgery, he was introduced to the sport of volleyball and developed skill quickly enough to hold his own with all-time greats of the sport such as Southern Californians Gene Selznick, Larry Rundle, and Ron Lang, all former U.S. Olympic team members. He formed an exhibition team with them—Wilt's Big Dippers—which once went 57 straight matches without defeat against first rate opposition.

He enjoys his physical prowess, and he hones it with weight-lifting, the volleyball, running, water skiing, swimming, and by romping with and training three huge Great Danes. Yet he glories in games such as chess and dominoes in which size and strength have no bearing at all. Real-estate holdings in California, New York, Pennsylvania, and elsewhere and an active stock portfolio attest to a mastery of the business world based on cunning, not on physique.

He is a world traveler, conversant with French, German, and Italian in addition to English, and he claims to have visited nearly 70 nations on basketball and vacation trips. Switzerland, he says, is the most beautiful of all.

Why is a man so accomplished and successful so widely despised?

Wilt Chamberlain, by *being* Wilt Chamberlain and by living as he does, represents proof of lesser men's shortcomings. Wilt Chamberlain *is* superior to most other men, and only individuals strong in their own egos and content within their identities find it no great task to forgive him for that superiority.

If he were *only* a star athlete . . . *only* a successful businessman . . . if *only* he had not so publicly achieved so much of what other men envy . . .

"Nobody roots for Goliath," he said. In a land full of self-styled Davids, that observation is all too true.

4

HAMLET IN SHORT PANTS:
NATE THURMOND

It was a night in April, one of those special evenings when just the right combination of damp and mist and cold makes San Francisco the best place in the world in which to be either very, very young or very, very old.

In the distance, through the huge picture window, the lights of the metropolis twinkled. Beyond them were the slow-moving dots of tugs and ferry boats and barges creeping across the bay.

Far, far away, Oakland sat in its gloom and grime, a cheerless, go-to-bed-early place brightened only now and then by an oasis of wee-morning-hours frivolity.

Music played softly, soulfully, through the stereo speakers and couples danced silently across the thick carpet while clusters of two and three and five long-valued, long-trusted friends and their handsome ladies talked about basketball games and about life, sipping good whisky and waiting for the dawn.

The talk became more philosophical and more heartfelt the closer it came to the hour of the sun's climb above the horizon, and people, black and white, drifted toward the door, one and two at a time, pausing to have a last word with the huge black man in whose apartment they'd been guests. Leaving that time and place where, for a night, time had suspended its relentless pace, they whispered their appreciation for warm hospitality and praised the man's courage and his skill.

An April night in a very beautiful San Francisco in 1967 . . . a night the Philadelphia 76ers defeated the San Francisco Warriors for the championship of the National Basketball Association . . . a night Wilt Chamberlain won his first world title . . . a night Nate Thurmond of the losing team held open house for his teammates, for his conquerors, and for his friends . . . a night a sportswriter named Harris, fortunate to have been invited to an all-night party, learned that a unique and precious love may exist among professional athletes. A night to treasure in a man's memory.

The Warriors, with reliable, earnest, self-effacing Nate the Great providing the integrity and fortitude and a brash sophomore pro named Rick Barry adding the explosiveness and furor, had forced the greatest team in history to six games of the final championship series before losing, 125-122.

Great as the 76ers were that season, a team with power and quickness and firepower and inspirational coaching, the Warriors had kept pace until late in each playoff game before losing four times, winning twice. The games were played ferociously, as only pro basketball playoff games are played, but there had been no squabbling and no petty bickering to mar the grandeur of the combat. Other title series before and since have not been played as cleanly or with equal freedom from tawdry interjections of ego and accusation.

Three years before, 7-foot-$1\frac{1}{16}$ Chamberlain had been the center for the Warriors, the most physically dominating player in the history of the sport. Thurmond, an awkward 6-foot-11 rookie, was asked to play forward.

They had practiced against each other, learned from each other, and had become friends. Chamberlain tutored the younger player not only on the fine points of being a giant playing this game for giants, but also in how to dress well and live well and travel well. He offered advice on means of coping with the pressures of their celebrity status and of their profession.

After the championship-deciding game at the huge, barn-like building known as the Cow Palace, Chamberlain and his protégé had embraced. They planned to meet after all the noise and confusion and pandemonium of the championship series conclusion ebbed. Nate invited Wilt and the 76ers to be his guests for an evening of season-end celebration.

And so they came, rivals with bonds of friendship greater than their athletic enmity, to Thurmond's luxurious apartment in one of San Francisco's lushest and most spectacularly view-blessed buildings. Some of Thurmond's non-basketball friends were there, too—married couples, bachelors, bachelorettes.

Nate circulated among his guests as unobtrusively as a man is able to if he is an inch under seven feet tall and if he weighs 230 pounds, seeing to it that no visitor went thirsty or neglected, seeing to it no bachelor stood alone if a bachelorette stood alone . . . seeing to it no one entered without greeting or departed without good-bye.

There was warmth there that night and a mutual regard and respect which was so good and so pervading you almost wanted to cry, it was so fine.

Yes, a special, very special night.

/ / /

At that moment, Nate Thurmond seemed on the threshold of greatness and acclaim even beyond what he had already achieved. He had become recognized clearly as the crown prince of basketball, better than Chamberlain defensively and better than the still-active Bill Russell offensively. He was an ideal combination of the two men's special talents.

With his quickness and long arms, his smooth outside shooting, his shot-blocking, rebounding, and willingness to sacrifice himself for the benefit of the team, he was the ideal center. He was heir apparent to Chamberlain and Russell as greatest among the great.

His fellow pros held him in awe as much for his quiet dignity and good humor and wit as for his ability to drive opposing teams to distraction. He was called "the best all-around center in basketball," and the Warriors, still young and blessed with talent at every position, were being called "pro basketball's next dynasty."

Eight years later, the great things which fortune seemed to have promised Thurmond and the Warriors finally were realized . . . but in bizarre fashion. In 1975, the Warriors finally became champions of the league, as Thurmond's guests that night anticipated. When it happened, however, Nate was unable to celebrate—he was nearing the end of his career as a member of the Chicago Bulls.

Rather than serving as the fulcrum for victory for the Warriors, he was sitting unhappily on the bench at Oakland Coliseum-Arena, a reserve, on May 14, 1975, when his former team defeated his new team, 83-79, in a tumultuous seventh game for the Western Conference championship. Two weeks later, the Warriors swept their fourth straight game from the heavily favored Washington Bullets in the most shocking title series the NBA has ever seen. The "dynasty" had been realized, but without Thurmond and only after eight intervening years of pain and frustration.

/ / /

Professional basketball began a great convulsion in the months following the 1967 championship series. A new league was organized in sputtering fits and starts which, for its first four years, made only a small dent in most NBA teams' fortunes . . . but which deeply wounded the Warriors.

Barry, the brilliant young forward whose slashing drives and outside jump shots had provided so telling a counterpoint to Thurmond's center play, became the first of only a handful of NBA players to respond to the American Basketball Association's siren call.

Barry decided to flee across the bay to an Oakland franchise organized by entertainer Pat Boone. Barry's father-in-law, Bruce Hale, was general manager and coach. Warrior owner Franklin J. Mieuli's necessary response was to enmesh Barry, himself, and the Warriors in a series of lawsuits and legal snarls which made enormous demands on his time and bank account.

Thurmond attempted manfully to carry both his and the departed Barry's burdens, but he was betrayed by his own body. He was stricken by one injury after another. The team floundered and became less and less interesting to fewer and fewer spectators.

The NBA, seeking to expand its horizons as well as its attractiveness to television networks, had grown from nine teams in 1965–66 to ten in 1966–67 with the addition of Chicago. Seattle and San Diego were added to the league the subsequent season, Phoenix and Milwaukee the season after that. There was no change in the lineup of franchises the following season, but the league's Board of Governors boldly—short-sightedly?—added Portland, Buffalo, and Cleveland to the league in 1970.

With each addition, expansion drafts took place in which existing teams made reserve players available to the newcomers. Each round of expansion reduced the league's general level of talent. Teams such as Boston, for instance, which once had been able to dip to their eighth and ninth men and find talented, experienced young veterans, now found men in those roles either aged and past their peaks or young and raw, so unready to play in the high-pressure, critical moments of games that they might not have survived even midsummer rookie tryout camps in pre-expansion days.

Another insidious trend, instigated as competition grew for college seniors' signatures in competition with the ABA, was the offering of "no cut" contracts. A youngster—guided by a high-priced negotiating agent in most instances—might demand, and receive, a contract guaranteeing a salary whether or not he was judged talented enough to help the team. Owners and general managers had the choice of retaining such players on their rosters or of cutting them, even though they would remain obligated to fulfill terms of their contracts.

The prevalent response, in evaluating an untried "no cut" rookie against a two- or three-year veteran reserve who had no such protection, was to keep the kid and drop the young-old pro, inasmuch as the youngster would have to be paid in either case.

The pattern throughout pro basketball became that teams consisted of cores of proven old-timers as starters, and another group, the high-priced, minimally productive rookies as infrequently used reserves.

The Warriors were not immune to this trend. But they suffered more than most teams because, as owner Mieuli

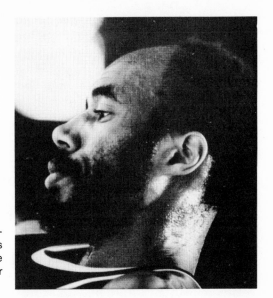

A brooding giant, Nate Thurmond pauses to catch his breath and consider the responsibilities he bears for the Golden State Warriors

concentrated on pursuing lawsuits and countersuits and devoted time to deposition-taking in hopes of regaining Barry's services, his front-office staff performed less and less successfully the tasks of scouting the college ranks and signing the men they drafted.

Coaches changed, Bill Sharman departing in 1968 in favor of journeyman ex-player George Lee, and Lee, in turn, being kicked upstairs to a part-time scouting job in favor of veteran guard Al Attles in 1970.

From April 1967 through the fall of 1973, the Warriors with Thurmond in the middle were, in a word, good enough to be regarded among the mid-rank of NBA teams, but not good enough to challenge for championships. They were good enough to be respected, but not good enough to lure many patrons to their games.

Mieuli, hailed in 1967 as an eccentric genius, became reviled in time as foolish . . . interested only in personal publicity. It was an unfair judgment, but, for better or worse, he was saddled with it.

Looked to for offensive as well as defensive leadership and

plagued by a series of injuries, Thurmond found himself plodding along. He was well paid, but earned his salary at the cost of pain and effort, wondering every time he took a shot or grabbed a rebound or blocked an opponent's field-goal attempt whether the effort might be too much for his brittle bones, his inflexible tendons and ligaments to survive. Each game was liable to be his last one, he admitted thinking, forced to the realization that he was an athlete unusually susceptible to injury.

Basketball became work for him at age 28 and 29 and 30 rather than a joy as it had been at 23, 24, and 25. A new generation of strong young giants came into the NBA, outrageously priced number-one draft choices, who matured and learned from the patterns established by Chamberlain, Russell, and Nate himself.

Thurmond came to be, in those middle years of his career, a sort of young elder statesman, regarded with warmth by other teams' executives and players, but without the flair or offcourt pyrotechnics which would have made him more celebrated.

Only in his succession of injuries did Thurmond become distinctive. He'd missed 4 games in his rookie season because of a back injury, 3 the next year (it should have been 30 games, but he forced himself to play despite the agony) with the same problem, 7 in 1965–66 because of a groin-muscle pull, 16 in the 1966–67 title season after suffering a broken hand which healed barely in time for the playoffs, 31 the next season with a major knee injury requiring surgery, 11 the next season because of an assortment of ills, and then the last 39 in the 1969–70 season when he suffered a second, even more painful and more serious knee injury.

That final disruption, coming at a time he was playing what might have been the finest basketball of his career, was a convulsive experience. Bitterly disappointed and convinced he was a man marked for doom, he called a press conference in his room at St. Mary's Hospital in San Francisco and announced he was quitting basketball—for the moment, anyway. He was serious, but he recanted the vow several weeks later.

The Warriors droned through a lost season, failing to reach

the playoffs without their star and establishing a pattern of boredom.

During the summer of 1970, Nate's topsy-turvy career turned from glory-touched but frustrating to merely frustrating. Mieuli, for reasons never explained and in shocking contrast to his previously notorious pampering of players, accused Thurmond of having malingered through what he claimed was an unnecessarily slow recovery. Mieuli accused Thurmond, too, of attempting to pressure him for an exorbitantly high salary after the injury by threatening to retire.

"I honestly think Nate would welcome getting injured in the first game he played after he signed this contract he wants," Mieuli complained at a lunch conversation with an astonished Wells Twombly, the award-winning sports columnist of the San Francisco *Examiner*.

"That way," Mieuli continued intently, a slight slur betraying the liquid phase of his meal, "it would cost me a million dollars to keep him in the life style he craves. Our team doctor tells us that his injury was not enough to keep him out for the rest of the season. Holding that press conference with forty games left killed our club's spirit. Nate was jockeying for position so he could hold me up for this contract demand.

"In seven years, Nate has shown only flashes of greatness. He breaks down every year, just when you need him most. In the off-season, he never touches a basketball and never seems to worry too much about getting into shape."

San Francisco fans, heretofore having heard only praise for Nate as a player and as a man, were aghast. "Franklin took a cheap shot," Thurmond responded with restraint. "To think that I would rather sit out than play is unbelievable. Why did he think I went through the pain and agony of an operation?

"It seems like he said all these things because he wants to justify trading me, like he is trying to disgrace me, put me down to the people who are my friends and fans.

"He doesn't pay me for the off-season. What I do is my business if I show up ready to play. I play forty-eight minutes a game. No one else has worked as hard. I don't think I've given him any indication I would rather sit out than play.

"In all the time I've been playing, this is the first detrimental article I've ever seen about myself."

The squabble became a bitter, prolonged contract dispute, and Nate held out the full preseason exhibition period. He finally signed a contract just before the opening of regular league play, reportedly for $150,000 per season for five years and with additional future, deferred salary. He worked himself slowly into shape as the season unreeled.

The knee continued to plague him, but he played with the pain, cautiously and without his former zeal, determined to give his team as much of himself as he could without succumbing once again to a major injury.

The fans turned on him for his holdout and for his conservatism. "Man how quickly the people forget," Nate said ruefully one night, noting with shock the boos directed at him by his own fans for the first time in his career. But he admitted he was playing with caution. "I'm doing more thinking out there on the floor now. I've stopped trying to overpower everybody," he confessed.

The knee injury which he'd thought would end his career had come as he dived to the floor to retrieve a loose ball. Now, he no longer dared be that selfless or that recklessly abandoned. "I don't think losing one game is as important as risking permanent injury," he admitted, in painful contrast to his earlier determination.

/ / /

Life had turned, despite his high salary and lavish bachelor life style, into a sort of gilded rat race. By the standards of society, he lived a luxurious kind of life. By the standards of athletics, however, where success is measured in championships and all-star-team recognition and with six-figure salaries so commonplace they are accepted as the rule rather than the exception, the gold was obscured by a thick tarnish.

If he was, as had been said of him, the crown prince among great centers, he was, like Shakespeare's Hamlet, self-doubting and troubled, aspiring but seemingly incapable of breaking loose from a pattern somehow decreed for him without his consent.

Asked once what his professional goal might be, Thurmond had responded, "To win a world championship and be voted the league's most valuable player." By 1971, as an elder statesman of the NBA and a battle-worn realist, his goal was much more modest. "I just hope to play all eighty-two games," he said with a sigh.

It seemed a plateau point in his career, a reaching of a high level without realistic optimism for a higher achievement. It was a time to reflect, on basketball and upon his life.

There was, first of all, his height. "Being a seven-footer puts you in a different world." he said ruefully. "I think that you have to condition yourself and your mind. You have to do something to live with it.

"Sometimes," he continued, looking back at his injuries and disappointments, "you have a depressed state. I do. I just want to go in a store and just pick up something that will freshen me all over. But this is impossible when you're seven feet tall.

"There are always uncomfortable things when you have a height such as mine. Being in cars, to a certain extent . . . it's very hard for me to drive a sports car. It's very difficult for me to relax properly when I'm flying in an airplane. Being a tall person and being noticed is something that some people have trouble coping with."

/ / /

The 1971–72 season was a turning point that neither Thurmond nor his teammates nor his management nor his city had a right to expect.

An off-season trade had brought 6-foot-5, high-scoring Cazzie Russell to the Warriors from the New York Knicks in exchange for rebounding specialist Jerry Lucas.

Lucas had come to the Warriors the previous year following an all-star career at Cincinnati and a dispute with Coach Bob Cousy. He was recovering physically from injuries, financially and emotionally from bankruptcy and the collapse of a million-dollar chain of Jerry Lucas Beef 'N' Shake franchises in Ohio. Expected to help Thurmond by providing scoring and rebounding, he'd continued injury-prone and unhappy instead.

Russell had been a regular once with the Knicks, but lost a starter's job to Bill Bradley when he was sidelined by a broken ankle and, returning from the injury, chafed on the bench. The Knicks sought a reserve center behind gimpy-legged Willis Reed and pursued Lucas for the role, offering Russell in trade.

Thurmond and 6-foot-9 Clyde Lee were among the league élite as rebounders, the previous season had demonstrated. What was needed was a quick, smaller forward who could fill the lane on the fast break and who could maneuver individually, one-on-one, to free himself for open shots . . . the role, in short, which Barry had performed for the club so brilliantly before turning to the ABA.

Thus, the Lucas-for-Russell deal was concluded and proved one of the rare transactions in sports history which truly benefited both teams. Lucas spelled Reed at times early in the season, then replaced him altogether when he was lost because of a new knee injury. And Russell provided instant offense, instant acceleration for a Warrior team desperately in need of precisely those things.

The Lakers compiled their incredible 33-game midseason win streak and won the over-all league championship, but the Warriors finished a respectable second behind them and at least reached the playoffs before succumbing to Kareem Abdul-Jabbar and the Milwaukee Bucks. But the evidence was clear—the Warriors' fortunes were finally reversing.

The next fall, the climb back to title contention was unexpectedly turned into a rocketing when Mieuli's long series of court fights for the services of Barry was rewarded. The 6-foot-7 former University of Miami All-American had become a member of the New York Nets by the fall of 1972, had become a part-time television sportscaster, had settled with his family on Long Island, and spoke of a new life in basketball, broadcasting, and business in his newest home city. Still, Mieuli had hope the courts would ultimately rule in his favor. He defied those who scoffed at him for pursuing a lost cause for so long. "I'm going East," he said a week before the 1972–73 season began, heading for the door, "to get my boy."

Mieuli's laugh was the loudest, a week later, when his seemingly hollow prediction came true. A Federal judge ruled in Mieuli's favor after all those years of confused litigation. After a six-year absence, Barry and his wife and family returned to the Bay Area. He was a Warrior once again. Mieuli had "gotten his boy."

Now it was Barry's and the other players' turn to go to work. Rick had to learn to play with the Warriors—only Thurmond,

Jeff Mullins, and Coach Attles remained on the club from his earlier career with the team—and they had to learn to play with him. It was a slow adjustment, but the addition of a bona fide All-Star made the Warriors a title threat.

There was reason once again for special exertion by all players. Freed from the obligation to work hard offensively in addition to continuing as the defensive hub, Thurmond returned to the controlled flamboyance of his younger days in the league. In a sense, he was reborn.

Barry's addition to the front-line depth meant that Attles could rotate his men more frequently. He could risk giving Thurmond breathers now and then because Lee could fill the gap. There was less need than at any time in the previous half-decade for Thurmond to pace himself. He was permitted, once again, to play as aggressively and with as much abandon as he could. The knee was always protected and the muscles creaked after stretches of two, three, and four games in a row, but the responsibilities for the welfare of the team were less and the opportunities for victory were more.

"They talk about the great combinations who have played together in this league," Thurmond said. "They talk about Jerry West and Elgin Baylor and they talk about Bob Cousy and Bill Russell. Rick and I should have been one of those great combinations. Certainly, I'm glad to have Rick back so we can now try to do all those things together, but that doesn't mean that I don't get sad thinking about the five years we wasted. We could have been in that group. We might have produced championships. Now we're finally getting our chance. But we're both getting older and we've both got bad knees."

Not until the postseason playoffs did the elements of the *new* Warriors come together completely. The Warriors were matched against Milwaukee again in the opening round, and the Midwest Division champions were heavily favored to eliminate the Warriors, only second behind Los Angeles in the Pacific Division. Instead of a Milwaukee sweep, however, the outcome was a victory by Golden State, four games to two, as Thurmond neutralized Abdul-Jabbar for the second straight playoff series.

"Nate plays me tougher than anybody else," admitted the

Milwaukee star as the upset loss to the Warriors touched off bewilderment and bitterness in Wisconsin. It had to be Milwaukee failure rather than Warrior skill which had decided the series. Hadn't it? Thurmond's knack for greatness without full recognition had manifested itself again.

Next came the Western Conference championship series against the world-champion Lakers.

Los Angeles players and their fans had followed the Milwaukee series with awe and accorded the Warriors appropriate respect. But the Lakers' superior cohesion and experience playing together in pressure situations was evident. In the opening game, for instance, Barry passed one way and Jim Barnett cut another on an in-bounds-pass situation in the

When you're a superstar center in pro basketball . . . like Nate Thurmond . . . you play hard even with a knee and thigh both heavily bandaged because of injuries which heal slowly

closing seconds to permit the Lakers a thrilling victory, 101-99. Two more Laker wins followed in succession before the Warriors prolonged the series with a 117-109 victory at their Oakland Coliseum-Arena home.

Play returned for game number five to the Lakers' home court, the Forum. The Lakers could relax with the quiet confidence of proven winners . . . and with a two-game cushion. The Warriors hadn't been winners for six years and their renaissance season would end with another defeat.

Although he'd promised himself two years earlier to be self-protective and cautious lest he risk an injury which might cripple him for life in so petty a cause as a basketball game, Thurmond played that night with all the fervor and intensity of his early career. He spared nothing of himself as he pitted his 6-foot-11, 235-pound frame against the power and mass of the Lakers' Chamberlain. They went rebound for rebound, blocked shot for blocked shot in a struggle that was truly titanic.

Early in the third period, Thurmond moved past the boundary of all-out effort into the screaming crimson area of danger.

He threw himself into a swirling tangle of arms and legs under the Laker basket, reaching for a missed Los Angeles field-goal attempt. He sought first to prevent the Lakers' Chamberlain or 6-foot-6, 230-pound Bill Bridges from converting the miss into a tap-in goal, second to get the ball for his own team. Other, smaller players entered the tangle. Thurmond managed to get his hands on the ball and slap it to a teammate, but fell heavily to the floor in the same sweep of effort.

After a momentary halt in play as fans and two sets of players murmured eerily in concern, he managed to get to his feet. It was obvious as he tried to continue that something was seriously wrong. Attles called for a time out and the trainer, Dick D'Oliva, came onto the court to take Thurmond by the arm and wrestle him to the locker room.

"I don't want to quit," the big man protested, his face dulled and glassy-eyed. "I don't want them to think I'm a quitter."

As he strode haltingly off the court and into the catacombs of the Forum, Thurmond was hailed spontaneously by his teammates, the Lakers, and 17,505 fans. All of them—professionals knowledgeable in the techniques of basketball and fans only vaguely aware of all that happens in a game—rose to accord Thurmond a prolonged standing ovation.

The Warriors trailed by 20 points at the time and would go on to lose, 128-118. Elimination from the playoffs once again. Disappointment again. "I was concerned for his health," Attles admitted later, explaining why he'd benched his most valuable player. "I didn't think the game was over at that point, but it may have been. That wouldn't have made any difference to me."

Said Thurmond afterward, slumped on the narrow bench in front of his locker in another gloomy postplayoff elimination scene, "I still don't know what happened. I kept asking what happened. I don't even remember playing after I got hit."

He flew home that night to San Francisco and was hospitalized overnight as a precaution, although his momentary blackout was nothing worse than a minor concussion sustained when Chamberlain's or Bridges' elbow smashed into his skull. The details had been blurred to observers by their swift occurrence, and Thurmond certainly had been so stunned he had no accurate picture of what had happened.

The season had ended, but 1973–74 beckoned alluringly as a continuation of the Barry-inspired resurgence of the franchise. And, in the next months, Thurmond's revived championship aspirations and new respect for the Warriors in the Bay Area helped remove some of the allegorical tarnish which, in Barry's absence, had marked his life.

What remained, in the summer of 1973 and in the season which followed, was the continuing puzzle of why Thurmond's greatness as an athlete has not earned him the same national fame and off-court financial rewards as have been enjoyed by Russell and Chamberlain among his contemporaries and by Abdul-Jabbar, Willis Reed, and Dave Cowens, among others, of a more recent vintage of NBA superstars.

/ / /

Barry, a former teammate and admirer, offers one explanation which makes too much sense to ignore. "Nate was never a big star in college, so he never got the publicity. The big men that come from college, like Russell or Wilt or Kareem, had big publicity and big reputations when they came to the pros. But Nate developed *in* the pros, so he was never really recognized."

The college was little Bowling Green in Ohio, to which he'd come at only 6-foot-7, a moderately regarded forward from the Central High School team in Akron which had starred a flashy and high-scoring future pro star named Gus Johnson.

Like Russell before him, Thurmond was a late maturer. The younger of two sons born to an employee at the Firestone tire plant, he continued to grow during his undergraduate days, reaching 6-foot-11 by his senior season. Unlike Russell, however, he was not the All-American and star of his team.

While Thurmond grew into his size and mastered the fundamentals of his sport, anonymously rebounding and playing defense and setting screens for his teammates, a 6-foot-2 left-handed-shooting guard named Howard Komives, a junior classman, was corralling attention as the nation's leading collegiate scorer.

Only the basketball buffs of the nation and only the scouts of the NBA knew Thurmond for what he was his senior season—the nation's best collegiate center. Was he, therefore, number one in the NBA draft? Would he gain, reaching the pro ranks, the surge of publicity that honor earns? Of course not.

The New York Knicks, in their prechampionship days, were a franchise encumbered by financial riches and unencumbered by athletic wisdom. Although reporters covering the team and their many knowledgeable fans pleaded that the Knicks needed a great big man to emerge as a playoff contender, the club used its rank as first team to draft to pluck a 6-foot-5 guard-forward from Duke University named Art Heyman. Originally from Long Island, Heyman was colorful and a high-scoring collegian with a reputation for fist-fighting and rambunctiousness. To the Knicks, he had a special attribute: he was Jewish, and the Knicks—in the seasons before their succession of sell-out crowds—had long sought a player who might become a special lure to New York's immense Jewish population.

The decision proved disastrous to both the Knicks and

Heyman himself, considering the pressure under which he tried to play. He became only an adequate pro at best, not big enough for greatness at forward and too slow for stardom at guard. His only strong suit remained eccentricity . . . to a degree which earned him regard in some circles, to this day, as honorary captain of the all-time Superflake All-Star Team.

The Warriors had second draft choice, having finished last in their half of the league following the move westward from Philadelphia and despite Chamberlain's personal heroics. The team had personnel deficiencies, but center was not one of them. The syndicate of San Francisco businesmen to whom Eddie Gottlieb had sold the team planned to follow conventional wisdom and draft anything *but* a center.

When the shock wave of the Knicks' selection of Heyman died away, the Warriors' brain trust wrestled with its dilemma. "Draft Thurmond anyway," Gottlieb urged sagely. "You just don't get big men like this coming along every year. Maybe he can play forward. If not, look what he could bring you in a trade!"

Thus, Thurmond embarked on his career not in New York, as had been anticipated, and where countless opportunities for endorsements and national publicity might have come his way, but in San Francisco, a city whose interest in pro basketball was still minimal and in which national publicity has always been difficult for athletes to attract.

"I was brought up in a hard-working, religious environment," says Thurmond, coping with his relative anonymity. "I'm black, but I'm also middle America. I never heard a religious slur in my whole life. I bought my parents a new home [in Akron] and a car, just like it says you're supposed to do when you hit it big in America. I own some real estate and I have some investments. I like to shoot pool and I don't drink much. I'm sort of a swinging square. I like solid things, you dig?

"I'm just not a tricky basketball player. Being flashy takes unnecessary effort. Once I got cute and tore up a leg muscle that kept me off the court for four weeks. I've had too many injuries to risk that sort of thing again. I suppose I could make a reputation for myself by dunking the ball and other stuff. But what would that get me?

"Over the years, injuries have nearly destroyed me. But I can't let those things slow me up. I'm a hard worker. I can't do it any other way. Some guys just seem to go out there and do things well. That's not my style. I have to study and learn. I have to outsmart my opponents, and that takes time.

"I'd love to be recognized for what I can do, not what others do to get themselves attention. I wish the writers would give me credit. The other players think I'm the best defensive big man in professional basketball. They're always coming up to me and saying that. Why would they lie? I'm sure they don't. I get the same reaction from other players that Bill Russell used to get. They acknowledge what I can do."

The style is, as Nate admits, subtle. While he has recovered his willingness to scramble for a loose ball or reach the extra foot or two for a rebound, he prefers to use self-control and position defensively. "I try to be like a pitcher on a batter," he says. "I've got a book on everybody that I play against. It's not written down, but it's in my head. Like a pitcher going over what to throw a batter on a three-and-two pitch, I go over what I have to do on my man. He has favorite moves, so before a game I sit down and take ten or fifteen minutes to think about what he likes to do. If I keep it fresh in my mind, I'll be looking for it and I'm one step ahead. Listen, defense is my game. If I don't keep up, I'll have to take a job selling insurance."

Offensively, he is equally unspectacular, yet effective. He has good inside moves, for one thing. He is not a high-percentage outside shooter, for another, but he has a soft, arching one-hander from 15 to 20 feet away from the basket which he uses to especially good effect when the defender matched against him stays too close to the basket.

A greater contribution than his outside shooting is his ability to flow with the offense. The ball comes in to him in the pivot and quickly returns to the outside or to a teammate cutting past him toward the basket. Having passed, he will step toward a defender and plant himself solidly, accepting countless bumps as men slam into him . . . and a teammate breaks into the clear for an open shot, the classic basketball "pick" play.

A forte, of course, is the rebound. Thurmond does not

crash men out of his way to reach the ball, nor does he soar effortlessly into the air, high above the basket, to pluck it insolently. He works at rebounding, grinding for position and then timing his jump, jumping again, if necessary, to get the ball. His quick and accurate passes started the Warriors' fast break and help the Bulls now as regularly as Russell's ever did for the Celtics.

His eyes are constantly alert, sweeping over the court to find the open space, to see which of his teammates might need defensive help. The jaw is slack with labored effort to catch fresh breath, the sinews and muscles etched visibly in three dimensions against the taut, sweat-shined skin. The expression changes little with the flow of the game, but there are command and leadership evident in him which exert themselves quietly and which account for the respect and affection of teammates and opponents alike.

"Nate is fantastic," says Jeff Mullins, whose career as the Warriors' highest-scoring guard was made possible largely through his ability to swing behind Thurmond's picks and screens to get free for open jump shots. "Nate's always willing to do whatever job he's assigned. And never with a fuss. If you want him to score twenty points, he'll do it. If you want him to forget shooting and concentrate on defense, well he's right there and no fuss. Always for the team."

/ / /

In 1974, at 33, Nate Thurmond was at his apex. Still a bachelor, pursued by and pursuing some of San Francisco's most charming young ladies, he was earning an estimated $250,000 per year or more and had invested in several promising enterprises including a soul-food restaurant in San Francisco's Fillmore District. He called the place The Beginning, and it ranks as eminently in its cuisine style as Ernie's or L'Etoile do among connoisseurs of the Continental. He drives a custom Rolls-Royce sedan and a spritely Datsun 240-Z roadster, both of which carry personalized license plates.

Forays into custom tailor shops and specialty stores dealing in quality sportswear for outsized men have made him one of San Francisco's best and most expensively dressed men. He moves with equal comfort through the Fillmore ghetto and through the Montgomery Street centers of high finance. He is universally known in San Francisco, universally liked.

But he no longer is a Warrior. Following the disappointment of the near-championship season of 1973–74, the Warriors underwent the most radical change of management and personnel since the club's transfer to the West Coast. Thurmond, seeking to expand his business interests and needing fresh capital to do so, asked to be traded to a team which would be willing to adjust his contract for greater immediate income, less money in the deferred payments which were due him after his retirement. The thought of trading Thurmond was appalling . . . but logical. He would have the opportunity, if the right deal could be made, to provide himself further lifetime security. The team would have the opportunity to reduce its payroll burden and funds might be added to the club's unhealthy bank balance if cash were made part of Thurmond's purchase price.

A new general manager, Dick Vertlieb, conferred with Mieuli. They discussed Thurmond's availability with several teams. The best offer was made by the Chicago Bulls—Thurmond for 6-foot-9 journeyman center, Clifford Ray, a future first-round draft choice, and a cash payment reported to be as much as $500,000. New York offered $1 million, but Vertlieb knew another center would be needed. Chicago offered one, the Knicks couldn't.

Chicago was tired of finishing second to Milwaukee and the great Kareem Abdul-Jabbar. A great center—Thurmond— would tip the balance of power, Coach Dick Motta pledged.

But the ensuing season proceeded in defiance of that pledge. Abdul-Jabbar was injured in the early weeks and Chicago managed, ultimately, to win the division title for the first time. But the younger, quicker Warriors refused to buckle before the Bulls' experience and depth when they met in the conference title series. Ray exhibited fierce intensity and leadership and shared center duty with lithe, inspired George Johnson to provide what teams normally achieve with just a single man. All twelve Warriors played roles in one rally after another as Golden State upset first Chicago and then the Washington Bullets to become NBA championships themselves, making a bitter mockery of Motta's pledge.

Thurmond had a pledge to make, too: he might play in

Chicago, but he would remain, by residence and in his postretirement life, a San Franciscan. That thought was reassuring to those in the Bay Area who regarded him with well-deserved warmth.

It is the character of the man that has built his image, not alone what he has done on basketball courts. He arose one evening to introduce himself, as had a sequence of guests at his table just before him, during a testimonial dinner in 1973 for Lon Simmons, a popular local sportscaster who was retiring from a longtime association with the San Francisco Giants. He unfolded from a chair designed for a shorter man and stretched elegantly to his full 6-foot-11. His expression was its familiar self-contained, semisomber, semimelancholy one.

But there was a sudden twinkle in his eye as he pronounced regally, "I, ladies and gentlemen, am Rodney Allen Rippey."

5

SEARCH FOR IDENTITY:
KAREEM ABDUL-JABBAR

He sat 20 rows back, well behind the home-team bench and in an elevated corner of the courtside-area seats. He was surrounded by the crowd, but his height and his skin color and an electricity of excitement made it clear he was not just another fan.

He sat uncomfortably. The head and shoulders were hunched forward—an unsuccessful attempt to disguise his size. The knees were tucked well under his chin because there was so little room for his long legs between rows of seats. The gestures were nervous. He looked straight ahead through deep-set eyes, now and then cupping his chin in a hand which seemed much too heavy to be supported by its slender wrist.

All around him, heads swiveled and fingers pointed in brief, furtive gestures. Whispers buzzed and, now and then, there were bursts of nervous giggling which had nothing to do with the game.

The gigantic young man, his hair close-cropped and his jaw showing a teen-ager's beginning of a wisp of a beard, pretended to ignore the looks directed at him and not to hear the whispers and snickers. But he had a haunted look, and he betrayed his discomfort by chewing furiously on a huge wad of gum.

He was a stranger in a strange land . . . Lew Alcindor, a freshman at UCLA visiting the Los Angeles Sports Arena for his first Los Angeles Lakers game and, at age 18, already a national celebrity.

He came now and then during the next four years to watch the Lakers play, on nights he did not have to play for UCLA and when studies did not interfere—and not even as a senior did he ever seem at ease.

Usually, he sat alone, aloof, silent, observing. Other college and high-school players from the area would come to games, too, and would cluster near the dressing rooms before tipoff time or during intermission to trade gossip, make boyish boasts, and leer at pretty girls. Alcindor acknowledged his contemporaries, but seldom joined them in their fun.

Sometimes, he wore his UCLA letterman's jacket. Otherwise, the clothes were dark-toned and correct, never flamboyant and never attracting additional attention to his towering height.

Sportswriters would approach from time to time to offer a hello, perhaps solicit a comment on a topic of the day. The answers were polite, well-considered, and articulate . . . but brief. He was not a young man eager to share of himself, but he was likable and he had a terrible earnestness about him that marked him as very, very special.

Sometimes, he would chuckle. But not often. Years later, he would observe, "I'm basically serious, but I laugh at a lot of things. People are funny. I'm not schizophrenic, it's just that most people relate to me either as a basketball player or as a seven-foot object . . . not as a person. That's what I have to deal with.

"I always was taller than other kids, but I was younger, too. You kind of withdraw in that situation. The things you don't know about, you let go by. After a while, it came to be my natural demeanor."

/ / /

Today, a decade after his first visit to a Laker game at their pre-Forum home, Lew Alcindor is an inch or two taller at what he insists is 7-foot-2, but reliably is reported at 7-foot-3

³⁄₈, and at least 30 pounds heavier at 235 than he was at 18. The close-cropped haircut of his youth has given way to a moderately full cut emphasizing with pride his African heritage and, in the style of his peers, he asserts an aspect of his manhood with a well-trimmed, mature beard.

The haunted look and the hesitancy to reveal too much of himself remain facets of his public character, however, and his name has changed from his original Ferdinand Lewis Alcindor, Jr., to Kareem Abdul-Jabbar in affirmation that he observes the Islamic religion of the Orient now rather than the Roman Catholicism of his youth.

The constant is his skill at basketball. He has been, in turn, the finest of the nation's high-school players, the finest of the nation's college players, and the finest of the nation's professional players. As each season of his career begins, he is expected to lead his team to a championship, and the wonder is that, despite the burden these expectations have been, he's succeeded at each increasingly challenging plateau.

Power Memorial Academy of New York City was regarded the nation's finest high-school team during his student days. UCLA, victor in a national sweepstakes to win his allegiance and matriculation, captured three consecutive national championships to establish a dynasty which has yet to crumble. And the Milwaukee Bucks have been among the most successful professional team in over-all numbers of victories against losses ever since he joined the NBA.

He is utter and total devastation on the basketball court. He is the tallest, most fluid, most intense, most sure-shooting, and most versatile of all the giants who have played the game.

His ability to score points with his swift moves and his soft shots distorts and influences a game so greatly that teams frequently resort to special strategies and schemes to stop him. Since basketball is a game which demands the split-second timing which comes only from game-earned experience, teams changing their tactics and lineups against Milwaukee only amplify whatever differences there may be already in the comparative talents of their personnel.

Some men have played alongside him and reached stardom although they have been too small or too slow to have been valuable in lineups unblessed by his special skills. Lynn Shackelford at UCLA, for example, minimized his slowness afoot, but emphasized his ability to hit the long, open shot, because opponents were forced to cope with Alcindor/Abdul-Jabbar in special ways.

On defense, Shackelford could crowd and overplay because Alcindor/Abdul-Jabbar's presence under the basket cut off the opposition's drive . . . a major, Bill Russell-originated way a big man, if he's agile, contributes to his team. On offense, as opponents sagged inward upon Alcindor/Abdul-Jabbar to prevent his free movement toward the basket, Shackelford could wait in his corner and then set himself for long, arching set shots relatively unbothered by the defense. He was an All-American collegian, but failed as a pro because, without a great center on his team, he could neither keep pace with men he was assigned to guard nor outmaneuver men assigned to guard him. Shackelford was not a strong rebounder, either—but, at UCLA, he did not have to be.

Jon McGlocklin has been valuable to Milwaukee for his outside shooting despite his lack of speed, and Milwaukee has won without outstanding forwards other than the clever Bob Dandridge because Abdul-Jabbar's greatness has been enough to compensate for his teammates' deficiencies.

Fascinating and dominating as his influence has been on basketball and no matter how firmly he is established as a premier superstar, Alcindor/Abdul-Jabbar's social role and personal growth may prove more far-reaching. Certainly, his personal history and his role in the national pattern of black self-assertion are more interesting to consider than his hook shots and rebounds.

/ / /

Four aspects of his life have made him introspective and sensitive. First, he is black. Second, he comes from the growing black middle class rather than from a personal history of ghetto deprivation; in this role, he is a minority member of a minority group. Third, he was raised a Roman Catholic. Fourth, less important in his social context, he is a giant forced to have made adjustments within his peer group because of his size.

In his era, Bill Russell was a bluntly outspoken black who used basketball as a route to personal assertion of manhood

The most unstoppable shot in pro basketball . . . Kareem Abdul-Jabbar's down-ward-thrown right-handed *sky hook* . . . arches over seven-foot Wilt Chamber-lain to swish through the netting and add points for the Milwaukee Bucks

and who used his position of power to reach into black communities as well as out to the white establishment. In his day, Wilt Chamberlain was so flamboyant, world-traveling, and pleasure-seeking a national personality that he was, somehow, above the question of race altogether—unique, protean, Olympian. But Alcindor, blessed by a richer early family life culturally than Russell, raised in the integrated Inwood district of Manhattan, and more academically oriented than either of his predecessors, was a questioner and a challenger early in his life. His generation sought to move from only acceptance of the Negro, assimilating and demanding equality, to the present forward thrust of black identity manifested as Black Power.

His answer, reached in inner turmoil at which he has only recently hinted, was religious.

Half a decade later, the answer for other young blacks struggling for identity and role might be political militancy and activism rather than the inward transformation of spiritual credo.

"My junior year at Power, when we were in the middle of a winning streak that was going to reach seventy-one games," Abdul-Jabbar recalled in a revealing autobiographical series in *Sports Illustrated* in 1970, "I was pretty close to the apex of my white-hating period. It seemed like every time I turned around, some white person was trying to push my face in the mud.

"One night, my friend Eric Brown and I went to a parish dance around Lexington and Sixtieth Street [in mid-town Manhattan], and as usual it was predominantly a white affair. We'd only been there a short time when Eric asked this white chick to dance and she automatically said no. Almost in the same breath she accepted a dance invitation from a white kid.

"There was something about the timing of it that enraged Eric and me. We stomped out of that place and began looking for trouble to cause. First we thought we'd punch out some store windows, so we headed over toward Times Square, and then we decided that we'd pick up some garbage cans and throw them through the windows on Fifth Avenue and all the time that we were making these plans we were walking faster and faster. Pretty soon, we'd walked off our rage. We rode home on the subway, thinking all the way.

"I still think about that night and I wonder how many of my black brothers have gone through the same situation, had their feelings hurt real bad and then went out and punched up some white person or maybe even killed somebody, all because of hurt feelings, like a little child, and never even knew why they were doing it.

"That blind rage is a part of the black condition; all black men reach it. Some pass through to a higher plateau of understanding, but some never get out of the rage period and their lives are blighted for it. I understand them, and I don't turn from them. I once felt that way myself."

The young man's rage and searching stemmed partly from his own experiences, and partly from the injustice he felt society had committed upon his mother and father. Musically gifted, they had met while members of a leading religious and theatrical choir, the Hall-Johnson Chorus, and his father had earned a degree at the famed Juilliard School of Music in New York. A trombonist at home in symphonic as well as popular music, the elder Alcindor accepted a civil-service career as security policeman in the New York City subway system because he found musical career opportunities closed to him because he was black.

/ / /

All that was known about Lew Alcindor . . . and all that most people *cared* to know about him . . . at that stage of his life was that he was an incredible basketball talent. Whichever college could enroll him as a student surely would come to dominate the sport, it was felt, and more than 200 schools and universities from all over the nation wooed him ceaselessly.

National magazines reported his exploits and nationally syndicated sportswriters sought him out for interviews while he was still a self-conscious, growing schoolboy. Chamberlain had provoked national attention at a similar age, but Power Memorial's location near the heart of New York City's communications centers and the growth of basketball publicity in the intervening decade made Alcindor far more prominent nationally.

His high-school coach, Jack Donahue, had screened interview requests from both news media and recruiters, but even
his assistance failed to reduce for the boy the full-time fluttering of the stomach and the blur of the mind that comes with
the necessity of making a difficult, life-setting decision.

Finally, on a morning in May 1965, the young man was
ready to announce his choice. He'd considered his parents'
hopes for him, considered climates and communities, considered coaches and programs. "This fall, I'll be attending UCLA
in Los Angeles," the earnest young man told a mob of nearly
100 radio, television, newspaper, and magazine reporters at a
press conference held in the Power Academy gym. "That's the
decision I came to," he said. "UCLA has everything I want in a
school."

The boy's disclosure made headlines all across the nation
and basketball people as well as the news media immediately
conceded UCLA the national championship for all three years
he'd be on the Bruin varsity. Enterprising reporters sought
out some pro coaches who chided the boy for planning to take
advantage of poor little college kids; he ought to go directly to
the NBA, they said.

UCLA's John Wooden, the scholarly, poetry-quoting former All-American from Purdue University whose teams had
dominated West Coast basketball for so long and who had
won NCAA championships with aggressive little teams in
1964 and 1965, didn't stand idle in the recruiting warfare
after getting Alcindor's commitment.

Shackelford had been a prep All-American at Burroughs
High in nearby, fabled Beautiful Downtown Burbank, and
another prep star was the swift and sturdy 6-foot-2 guard
from Wyandotte High of Kansas City, Lucius Allen. Wooden's
staff attracted Shackelford, and Wooden himself enticed
Allen after meeting him at a Fellowship of Christian Athletes
conference. Also drawn to UCLA was a bespectacled, slightly
built 6-foot-3 youngster from Santa Maria in central California, Ken Heitz, who'd also been ranked one of the nation's
finest high-school players.

It was an astounding collection of talent. An alumni association committeeman named H. R. Haldeman, a local advertis-
ing executive with an interest in politics, had headed a fund-

raising campaign for the construction of a 13,000-plus-seat new arena on campus, and the thought of what Alcindor and his fellow freshmen might accomplish in the new building had UCLA fans salivating eagerly in anticipation.

The first event ever to be staged in the new facility, Pauley Pavilion, would be Coach Wooden's annual climax to preseason training: a game between the frosh and the varsity . . . the defending national-champion varsity . . . the ranked-first-in-the-country varsity. Alcindor scored 31 points for the yearlings in a 75-60 rout and it was duly noted thereafter that UCLA was ranked number one in the country, but only number two on its own campus!

Games against local junior-college and freshman teams were mockeries that season. Alcindor, Allen, Shackelford, and Heitz played only long enough to insure victory before non-scholarship youngsters came onto the floor to complete avalanche-scaled romps. The only competition for the team came in scrimmages against the varsity.

For Alcindor, still physically frail and immature, the only individual competition came in one-on-one work each practice session with a former Oregon State star named Jay Carty, rough and tough and 6-foot-8, whom Wooden hired out of the UCLA graduate school especially to provide special, physically punishing schooling for his *wunderkind*.

The first year in college is a difficult transition for even the most mature youngsters. Alcindor was adjusting not only to basketball, but also to a new city and a new culture. He could go nowhere without attracting attention and he sought unsuccessfully for the kind of fun he saw other freshmen enjoying.

"I quickly discovered that there is a special breed of people called Californians," he would recall later, "with their own culture and background and attitudes. I discovered that most Californians came from other places where racial prejudice abounded, and some of these Californians had the same feelings about race as their friends back home. To these bigoted people, deep down inside, I was nothing but a 'jive nigger.'

"There also seems to be a special art form in California. It's the art of seeming to like people that you really don't like. It wasn't long before I realized that certain cats who hated my

Using every bit of his 7-foot-3⅜ height, Kareem Abdul-Jabbar reaches toward the sky for firm two-handed defensive rebound despite frantic efforts of Boston's 6-foot-8 Dave Cowens during 1973–74 NBA championship playoffs

guts were giving me big smiles and saying, 'Hello, how are you?' People here have absolutely no commitment to you whatever."

The adjustment from the hustle-bustle, aggressively candid, and compressed life style of New York City to the urban sprawl and insular attitudes of Southern California was difficult.

"In New York, my situation was always a pretty well-defined thing," he said. "I went to school, I came home, I played basketball, I had my friends, I went to camp in the summer.

"Being in California gave me a new perspective. I met new people, discovered new concepts. I didn't feel lost in California as much as I felt alienated. California runs a game on the rest of the country. It pretends to be liberal, but it is not liberal. Look at what happens in their elections. There are phony people there. I doubt the people are for real.

"They think I'm moody and reclusive, but under these conditions that's the only way I can be. The people here don't know what is going on around them. I'm disappointed in the atmosphere here. Most of the students seem out of it. They do not know how people in the rest of the world live. They have a limited point of view as opposed to New York City."

On court, the freshman seemed uninterested, almost insolently unconcerned. There seemed no emotion at all on his face as, chewing on his Juicy Fruit, he swatted down the other teams' layup attempts or reached in textbook-pure moves over outsized opponents to drop hook shots into the basket.

Rumors of his dissatisfaction with UCLA and of his allegedly militant racial attitudes circulated widely in Southern California, I recall. There seemed to be even a mathematical relationship between strength of rumors and success of the team—the better Alcindor played, the more rumbles there seemed to be about his plans to transfer to another school.

A cloak of silence had been swirled around Alcindor by Wooden and UCLA officials. Interview requests were turned down with the explanation that UCLA policy had long been to disallow interviews with freshman athletes. It was a justifiable policy, perhaps, but no one in the Southern California media corps could remember its having been previously invoked. The prevalent view was that Alcindor had asked for the publicity screen, and his alienation from reporters and the public was all the greater as a result. Only later did he reveal that the interview ban had been UCLA's idea, not his.

It was a questioning time in his life . . . as it is for all young men. His education had been through parochial schools operated by various orders of Roman Catholic clergy until he came to UCLA. He'd learned one set of religious values, one set of social truths, one set of biases and hates of his own. Three thousand miles away from his roots, he began to re-examine ideas and emotions in light of new movements and new issues.

He read, among other books, *The Autobiography of Malcolm X*, the one-time chief lieutenant of Elijah Muhammad, the former Elijah Poole, "messenger of Allah" and leader of what he called the New Lost-Found Nation of Islam in the West. The group, estimated at up to half a million strong, is known in America as the Black Muslims. A first burst of wide national attention came in 1964 through the conversion to its teachings of heavyweight boxing champion Cassius Clay . . . Muhammad Ali.

A self-confessed former pimp, drug addict, prison inmate, hustler, and white-hater from Boston, Malcolm Little had found a goal and direction preaching the gospel of black supremacy, black separatism, and black purity of Elijah Muhammad's sect under the Muslim name Malcolm X—a rejection of the slave name Little.

The holy text was the *Koran*, but Elijah Muhammad had added elements of theology and hatred for whites unheard of in any mosque of orthodox Islam anywhere else in the world.

As Malcolm's role as chief public spokesman for these views brought him greater attention, his own questioning had grown. He sought formal ties with orthodox, international Islamic traditions and made a pilgrimage to the Holy City of Mecca in 1964 which modified his views profoundly.

Rather than fulfilling his objective of gaining recognition for the Elijah Muhammad group within Islam, Malcolm found—he wrote later—a reaching out and a brotherhood among Arabic Moslems which transcended skin color. In an act which would have profound impact on millions of lives, he broke with his former teacher and adopted the formal Moslem teachings and theology of millions of Middle-Eastern and Asian members of the Sunnite sect.

Establishing a new following and diverting membership from Elijah Muhammad, Malcolm wrote his life story and began preaching against, rather than in favor of, racial hatred. His emphasis remained black solidarity and black pride, however.

As he delivered one such message at a meeting of his Muslim Mosque, Inc. in the Audubon Ballroom in Manhattan's Harlem on February 21, 1965, he was assassinated by blacks believed—but never proven to be—members of the Elijah Muhammad faction. It was a martyrdom which made Malcolm's self-discoveries and new world-view all the more compelling.

Young blacks might seek new values and might seek to disavow Christianity as a "white man's religion," but here was a way to do so within the framework of a sophisticated theology and culture more than a thousand years old.

Lew Alcindor, reading Malcolm's life story, sought the same enlightenment. "Malcolm was a Sunnite Moslem when he was killed and his story was an inspiration for me. I had to investigate," he said later. "I saw how he had used [Islam] to help himself grow."

The word was spread—albeit in whispers—in Southern California that Lew Alcindor had become a Black Muslim. His seeming hostility to news media and the quietly, unemotionally ferocious style of his play made the stories believable to those who perhaps underestimated his intellect or failed to research sufficiently the convoluted set of beliefs that membership in the Nation of Islam would have involved.

For ghetto blacks with little inner pride and little prospects of financial advance, Elijah Muhammad offered a self-discipline and self-esteem which was vital and appealing. But the story of a messenger of Allah named W. D. Fard and the idea of *all* white men as "blue-eyed devils" would not so easily be accepted by a serious-minded, intellectually inquisitive youngster with a sophisticated background, those of us in Los Angeles who admired Lew Alcindor felt. (Muhammad's leadership role passed to his son, Wallace, upon his death in 1975, and one of Wallace Muhammad's first steps was to soften the "devil" accusation against whites.)

Only later, as he left UCLA to begin his professional career, did he explain his evolution from black rage to black pride through Sunnite teachings and affiliation with a group of Malcolm's disciples.

"I could no longer believe," he said, "that the white man was inherently evil and cruel and black men inherently superior, as some blacks are teaching nowadays. That is just the flip side of the old racism. I realized that black was neither best nor worst—it just was. I could no longer hate anybody. I could no longer afford to be a racist. If racism messed up a lot of people who had to take it, then it must also mess up those who had to dish it out. I did not want to be that kind of narrow man."

The searching and the reaching out came during Alcindor's sophomore and junior seasons at UCLA, while the rumors of his alleged black-nationalist convictions continued. On the court, orthodoxy meant only to perform faithfully and enthusiastically the maneuvers Coach Wooden might demand. Faithful adherence to the coach's instructions for crisp passing, aggressive defense, energetic rebounding was unfailingly rewarded with victory.

Basketball was an outlet and a haven from the tortures of inner doubts. Junior guard Mike Warren provided experience and floor direction for sophomores Alcindor, Shackelford, Heitz, and Allen, and the Bruins won, as expected, 30 consecutive games for a perfect season . . . and a national championship.

That same group, augmented by additional, incoming talents, continued with 17 straight victories at the start of the 1967–68 season. Then came an epic loss on January 20, 1968, to the University of Houston at the Astrodome in Texas, 71-69. The game drew basketball's all-time largest crowd—52, 693—as well as a huge national television audience. Alcindor played that night with a scratched eyeball, suffered in a win over California a week earlier, which blurred the vision in his left eye.

Vindication for the loss came three months later in the NCAA semifinals when the Bruins humiliated Houston, 101-69, at the Los Angeles Sports Arena. Alcindor, usually so stoic and apparently unemotional on the court, sprinted out for the opening lineup introductions that night and slapped hands *soul* style with previously introduced teammates with great animation. After an exceptionally clever pass from Warren to Shackelford which resulted in a field goal early in the game, Alcindor raised two huge fists and shook them in excitement. The rematch and the opportunity to play again against Houston's star, 6-foot-9 center Elvin Hayes, was obviously especially motivating.

Basketball's rules-makers had outlawed an Alcindor specialty—the dunk shot—following his sophomore season. Had they not deprived him of this special act of self-expression, surely that night he'd have dunked some mighty dunks indeed.

A championship-game victory over North Carolina the next night, 78-55, was almost an anticlimax as UCLA won its fourth NCAA crown, and the only blot on the Bruins' record the next season, enroute to national title number five, was a meaningless loss to USC more than a week after the conference title was safely tucked away.

In three varsity seasons, UCLA won 88 games and lost only two! The University of San Francisco's Bill Russell-inspired run of 55 consecutive victories was intact, but not even the Russell-led Dons had dominated college basketball so completely for so long.

Alcindor finished his UCLA career as the school's all-time leading scorer, all-time rebound leader, all-time high-percentage shooter, all-time holder of dozens of one-game, one-season, and pavilion records. The points and the statistics came without special effort at individual achievement, for that was not Wooden's way, nor Alcindor's. A product of the intense crucible of New York City schoolboy play and then refined under Wooden's discipline, Lew was the ultimate team player.

"I don't mind passing," he said. "The job here is to win. It would be selfish of me to force a shot if any of the team were clear. I'll take my shots if I can, but that doesn't happen very often. So I pass off and we make easy baskets, and I try to do my best in rebounding because that leads to more easy scoring chances."

This winning attitude was gratifying to Wooden even as he fretted and fumed at the demands Bruin fans made that his team win more convincingly, more spectacularly each night. "He doesn't hesitate to pass," said Wooden, "and he realizes his value to the team when he does. He is an unselfish player who does what has to be done to get another win.

"But he is very reassuring on your side when the other team begins catching up because he always seems to have his best games under pressure.

"When we absolutely need a basket or a rebound, or when it becomes crucial to stop the other team from scoring, Lewis finds a way to do it.

"The others admire him for this. He could easily have taken to dominating the offense, and who would have been able to stop him if he wanted to score fifty or sixty points every game? But it's better this way. Much better."

The American Basketball Association, founded on short money and long hopes in 1966, had talked endlessly about the huge, overwhelming financial offer it would make to Alcindor when he became eligible for the pro draft. The NBA, older and secure with that maturity, made lesser boasts, but was prepared to act boldly, too. Alcindor's talents would turn the team which drafted him into a title contender instantly, and, beyond simply his on-court skills, the propaganda value to the league which signed him would be immense.

Advised and assisted by a wealthy Southern California contractor who was special friend and advisor, without financial compensation, to many UCLA athletes, Sam Gilbert, Alcindor arranged to meet with representatives of the two leagues.

The NBA resisted rumors that Alcindor, supposedly alienated by Southern California and supposedly determined to live in a metropolis, would refuse to sign with either of the two teams which would contend for the right to negotiate with him—expansion franchises Milwaukee and Phoenix.

Under NBA procedure, the two teams with the respective poorest records in the Eastern and Western Divisions would flip a coin for first draft choice. The prospect of opportunity to draft Alcindor had been among considerations of both management groups when they plunked down more than $1 million each for their original franchises.

Not even Nate Thurmond's height is enough to prevent defensive block by Milwaukee's Kareem Abdul-Jabbar

Phoenix conducted a season-long promotion campaign urging fans to vote either "heads" or "tails" as the call on the day of decision—March 19, 1968. Commissioner J. Walter Kennedy flipped a special coin in his New York office while Presidents Richard Bloch of the Suns and Wesley Pavalon of the Bucks, in their respective cities, waited by their telephones.

"Heads," Bloch called in response to the vote of his city's fans.

"It's tails," Commissioner Kennedy announced.

The ABA resorted to no such chancy a procedure. Desperate to land Alcindor and the prestige he'd bring with him, the league agreed that Arthur Brown, a trucking-firm executive and owner of the Long Island-based New York Nets, should seek out the UCLA star. To heck with the formality of a draft.

Said Alcindor, "I will accept only one offer from each team, and I will then choose the better one with the help of my advisors. I will not engage in any extended negotiating that would lead to a long-drawn-out newspaper circus, and I do not want to make enemies of anyone."

The meetings took place and Alcindor, advised by Gilbert and another friend, Ralph Shapiro, heard them out. Milwaukee offered a $1.4 million package including direct salary, bonus, insurance policies, and other considerations. Brown and ABA Commissioner George Mikan offered $1 million—$200,000 per season for five seasons.

Admitting he'd wished the Nets' offer had been better, as ABA people had boasted it would be, so that he could play in New York, Alcindor announced he would sign with Milwaukee. The ABA hastily convened to offer a second proposal totaling more than $3 million, but the towering youngster refused to go back on his word. In 1975 there was a new furor over his wanting to leave Milwaukee—which he admitted while insisting he would fulfill his contract.

"If I had a hundred choices of where I wanted to play," he said, "ninety-nine of them would have been New York. But I accepted the NBA offer because it was more solid."

It was in the span between his signing with Milwaukee and his official NBA debut against Detroit on October 18, 1968 (in a game televised nationally on ABC's Wide World of Sports) that Kareem agreed to a three-part autobiographical series to appear in *Sports Illustrated*. A sensitive writer, Jack Olsen, was assigned to turn Kareem's tape-recorded words into manuscript and the athlete would be paid $20,000. In the series, he revealed formally and officially that he had adopted the Islamic faith ("I had my Islamic baptism, my *shahada,* after my junior year") and the Islamic name Kareem Abdul-Jabbar.

/ / /

His rookie season in the NBA was as much a revelation as had been predicted, although some of the anticipation which had grown over the summer was dampened at Bill Russell's off-season retirement and an injury to Wilt Chamberlain that prevented the two giants from playing more than just one early-season game against each other. In that one game, at the Forum in Southern California, Milwaukee lost while Chamberlain and the young giant played to a standoff.

Their first season in the NBA, the Bucks had won only 27 games and lost nearly $400,000. After adding Alcindor—who still used that name publicly—they climbed to 56 wins in 1969–70 and second place in the East behind only the world-champion New York Knicks. The financial gain for the franchise was just as startling as the improved win-loss record.

If Alcindor had a weakness, it was that, still growing into his height, he wasn't a dominating rebounder in the style of Chamberlain or smaller rivals Nate Thurmond, Elvin Hayes, and Wes Unseld.

By the 1970–71 season, he'd added strength . . . and a new teammate, Oscar Robertson, a 12-year All-Pro regarded as the finest guard of all time. Oscar became available when a rival for that title, ex-Celtic Bob Cousy, became coach of the Cincinnati Royals and attempted—unsuccessfully, as it turned out—to remake the Royals in the Celtic image.

The combination of Robertson's floor direction and Alcindor's all-around pivot play, interworking in cleverly conceived offenses and defenses designed by an aggressive young coach, Larry Costello, proved devastating. The other players were no better than just pro journeymen, but with Robertson and Alcindor there to magnify and augment their skills, they were good enough. The Bucks won 66 games, lost only 16, and enriched the franchise treasury enormously en route to the world championship. It took only five games to dispose of San Francisco and then Los Angeles in the first two playoff series, then just four to humiliate the Baltimore Bullets for the title.

It was shortly after the close of the championship series that Lew Alcindor finally, publicly, historically became Kareem Abdul-Jabbar.

He married the former Janice Brown of Los Angeles, who had taken the name Habiba, in May in Washington, D.C., in a traditional four a.m. Islamic ceremony. They honeymooned briefly, and then joined Costello, Robertson, and several other Bucks and their wives in Washington, D.C., on June 3, 1971, for a final briefing before a State Department-sponsored tour of Africa.

A news conference was staged, and Lew Alcindor stood tall in an impeccably tailored white knit suit to announce, "I've been kind of quiet about it up to now, but now that I'm representing this country, I want to do it. When I'm speaking to people and holding news conferences [in Africa], I want to use my Islamic name."

Thus, exit Ferdinand Lewis Alcindor, Jr., enter Kareem Abdul-Jabbar, a name fulfilling Islamic doctrine in that all believers "bear a name of Allah," or a paraphrase thereof, and also a name which characterized its bearer.

"Kareem means 'noble or generous,'" he explained. "Abdul is 'servant of Allah' and Jabbar means 'powerful.'" The name was given him by the Hanafi-Sunnite sect leader, Hamaas Abdul-Khaalis, successor in leadership to Malcolm X and, like Malcolm, a spurner of the preachings of Elijah Muhammad.

The amazing thing about Kareem's announcement was that, seven years after the derision which had greeted Cassius Clay's request that the public recognize him as Muhammad Ali, the basketball player's announcement should be accepted so soon.

The swiftness of transition was made forcefully apparent the following September, when Milwaukee opened the defense of its world title with an exhibition-game series against the Phoenix Suns and Los Angeles Lakers in Honolulu.

There were a few guffaws and catcalls from the rafters of Honolulu International Center as, in pregame introductions, the public-address announcer intoned, "From UCLA, wearing number thirty-three, formerly known as Lew Alcindor . . . KAREEM ABDUL-JABBAR!" Otherwise, the introduction drew the kind of applause the league's Most Valuable Player deserved.

The clincher, however, came after less than two minutes of the game had been played. Jon McGlocklin, the relatively molasses-footed guard who had become accustomed to getting shooting room because opponents persisted in collapsing in the middle against the huge center, cut through the key on a routine play and realized suddenly that he'd shaken free of his defender. "Kareem," he screamed instantly, "I'm open in the corner!"

That a teammate should adopt the new name in such a moment—as early in the season as the first game played by Kareem Abdul-Jabbar—was undeniable proof that the new name would be accepted universally. That view was confirmed frequently in the next weeks as pro basketball people gathered to consider ways to defend against him . . . and referred to him as "Kareem" or "Abdul-Jabbar" even in their private conversations.

The Bucks repeated as Midwest Division champions the next two seasons, winning over 60 games each year despite injuries to key men. They lost to Chamberlain and the record-setting Lakers in 1971–72 in the Western Conference playoff finals and were upset in 1972–73 by Thurmond and the Golden State Warriors in the conference semis.

Abdul-Jabbar refused to offer excuses, but it was a paramount factor in 1972–73 that he lived from January through May in virtual seclusion and under constant armed guard. Thugs—suspected of being Black Muslims—attacked the Washington, D.C., Hanafi sect headquarters (mosque and living quarters) he'd purchased on behalf of the group, and murdered seven of Khaalis' disciples.

It was grisly and horrible, and the terror was rekindled each night as the sect's best-known member played basketball and detectives armed with pistols sat alertly behind the Milwaukee bench lest rumored assassination threats against him be carried out.

"You will never hear me put the knock on another black

man," Kareem Abdul-Jabbar said, proclaiming he had no hatred to bear toward the Black Muslims or toward anyone else. "Black people already have enough burdens to bear. Just let me say that I found Elijah's religion too narrow, too negative and, in my opinion, not truly Muslim at all.

"The genuine Muslim bears witness that there is one God, that his name is Allah, and that all men—black and white—are brothers. There is no room in Islam for racial hatred of any sort, and I came to realize that this was exactly the way I felt in my heart. I worked past the age of rage."

Later, four men from Philadelphia were apprehended, charged, and, ultimately, convicted of the mass murders in Washington, D.C. A fifth suspect was acquitted. The five men were Muslims, but there was no accusation that they had committed the murders under any motivations other than their own grotesquely misdirected loyalties to their sect's leaders.

For Kareem Abdul-Jabbar, the arrests meant resolved anxieties and tensions. There would be no more bodyguards, no more subterfuges and uncomfortable travel arrangements to assure his safety. In an improved 1973–74 NBA, Milwaukee compiled the league's best win-loss record and the Bucks' brilliant center was voted Most Valuable Player in the NBA for the third time in his career. In 1974–75, he began wearing special goggles after a preseason eye injury, and Milwaukee rebuilt its guard corps following Robertson's retirement. It was a down year for the team, but his individual reputation was not diminished.

Loping downcourt in huge strides, setting himself in his favored position on the left side of the basket, near the hoop, and then looking up to accept passes from teammates, Kareem Abdul-Jabbar and his short, soft, downward-hurtling right-handed hook shot—his sky hook—have become ultimate basketball weapons.

"Hmm," murmured Bill Russell back when he was a national telecaster watching his young successor as most dominant player in the NBA, "that's a mighty high percentage shot."

Allah be praised.

Kareem Abdul-Jabbar be praised, too.

6

THE GIMPY-LEGGED LEADER:
WILLIS REED

The sound was born up near the roof, in those distant seats fully nine floors above the grime and churning humanity of Seventh Avenue in midtown Manhattan. The bulk of Willis Reed was seen emerging from a corridor exit to move in painful lurches down a flight of steps to the basketball floor. There must have been that one first observer and that one first shout from one first exhilarated fan ... but history provides no record quite that precise.

From that original anonymous cheer grew the united crescendo of 19,694 men, women, and children greeting, as if as one, the appearance of a truly charismatic hero. It was a volume of sound, it seemed, that threatened to jostle the mass of Madison Square Garden off its very foundations. . . perhaps shake the entire island ... lift an entire metropolis. . . .

It was May 7, 1970. Pain-killing injections numbing the scream of torn muscles in his right thigh—and robbing him of sensation from hip to toe—Reed reached the playing floor to join the New York Knicks for combat with the Los Angeles Lakers in the deciding seventh game of the NBA championship playoffs.

It was the closest New York ever had come to winning the title in the sport it claimed as its own special heritage. Without Reed's 6-foot-10, 245-pound bulk to combat the strength and domination of the Lakers' Wilt Chamberlain, there could be no victory. With no victory, there could be no title.

"Those weren't nineteen thousand spectators," recalled former Rhodes scholar Bill Bradley, one of the Knicks' forwards, later, "they were nineteen thousand *participants*. When they pulled down the roof for Willis, it lifted us sky high."

Reed, the captain of the team, was able to move only with the agility of a bull elephant in its death throes. But the inspirational force of his halting, heroic emergence from the training room and onto the court was self-evident. New assurance spread somehow among his teammates. He managed to lift himself high enough, early in the game, to find the basket twice with his soft, left-handed jump shot . . . if only off his toetips rather than with his normal leap. Limping awkwardly and mechanically, he interposed himself between Chamberlain and the basketball well enough at least to neutralize the great Los Angeles star and force his team to desert its favorite tactics.

Quickly, the game became one-sided. New York became the winner . . . the series winner . . . the world champion. The final score was 113-99. So emotionally and effectively did the Knicks perform after the appearance of their leader, it might as easily have been 213-99.

"I've never played with as much pain," said Reed, perspiration boiling off his dramatically etched ebony face, "but this was one game I had to play. I had to be part of it. I have all summer to recover."

Each time Reed lumbered between Chamberlain and the basket, permitting Dave DeBusschere or Walt Frazier or some other New Yorker to get a rebound, the crowd roared anew.

Each time Frazier flicked out his quick hands to deflect a Laker dribble and race downcourt unmolested for a layup, there was more pandemonium.

But no noise that night, perhaps no noise ever heard in the history of games played in enclosed arenas, matched the outpouring of sheer, raw, joyous emotion which was triggered by Reed's appearance and declaration he would play.

/ / /

The game remains a watershed moment for pro basketball.

The Knicks' victory was the culmination of a long love affair between a basketball-mad city and its team. For years an embarrassment to the NBA because they were so inept a group in its most important franchise city, the Knicks had evolved in time into a contending unit and, in their magic season, at last into champions.

Each game of the championship series, midweek nights as well as Sunday afternoons, was nationally telecast for the first time in league history, a match not only of teams from Los Angeles and New York but also of those two great, dissimilar cities. The focus of attention from newspapers, magazines, radio, television, and book publishing on the title series was greater by far than anything pro basketball had ever known before.

New York's ghetto people and garment-district people and Bronx people and Brooklyn people had known and grown up with basketball.

Because the Knicks had galvanized their city so excitingly that season, the men on Madison Avenue and Wall Street began, suddenly, to know basketball, too. Knicks began appearing on the late-night talk shows, in the magazine ads, on network commercials.

Poor Donnie May, one of the subs. He didn't use the right hair tonic, according to an endlessly replayed TV mini-drama starring the entire team, and Willis Reed refused to let him touch the ball! For shame, Donnie May. No more greasy kid stuff for you!

Pro basketball became, after a quarter century of floundering struggle and petty bickering among men of limited bankrolls and proportionate ambitions, a national topic. Not long afterward, pro basketball players emerged as the élite of professional athletes financially. By 1974, a newly granted franchise for the city of New Orleans would cost $6.15 million. Only 12 years before, NBA pioneer Eddie Gottlieb of Philadelphia, in startling contrast, consented to selling his Warriors to a group of Californians because they were citing the huge, windfall price of $800,000 . . . an offer far too astounding to be refused.

Had the Knicks of 1969–70 simply gone out and whipped Los Angeles for the championship, it would have been enough. The revolution in respect for pro basketball might still have occurred. The joy of the New Yorker at success in his favorite sport would still have been supreme.

To win with such drama and with such display of individual courage by so well beloved a man as Reed, though, made the triumph all the more memorable.

A product of tiny Bernice, Louisiana, and of Grambling College, a school much better known for its contributions to pro football than for its basketball successes (and better known for its contributions to sport than for its contributions to life in the rural South, alas), Reed was a symbol for the growth of the Knicks from miserable also-rans to champions. It was against the Knicks, it should be remembered, that Chamberlain had recorded his 100-point game in 1962, and the unprecedented individual achievement astounded New York fans as much as it amazed other basketball followers . . . but galled them, too, because it so clearly demonstrated the futility of their team.

Reed joined the Knicks two years later. He was a fixture in the growth seasons of 1964–65 through 1968–69. And he was the hub of offense and defense in 1969–70 as awareness grew and snowballed through a glorious season that the best was still to come. In November and December, the Knicks reeled off 19 consecutive victories, an NBA record at the time. The victories continued to pile up, and soon the Eastern Division championship was assured . . . a significant milestone.

The playoffs came and New York disposed of Baltimore in an exhausting seven-game preliminary series, then whipped Milwaukee in just five games for the division crown, despite the Bucks' brilliant rookie, Lew Alcindor. This was milestone number two.

The Western Division competition, meanwhile, was greatly overshadowed by the Knicks' exploits. Atlanta had won the regular season title during Chamberlain's convalescence from a November knee injury. Chicago finished third in the race, Phoenix fourth. In the playoffs, Wilt returned to the Los Angeles lineup, leading the Lakers past Phoenix as Atlanta disposed of Chicago. And then the Lakers toppled Atlanta in

Pain and sweat wash away
for Willis Reed when he
showers following a New
York Knicks playoff game
victory

four straight games to earn the championship round against
New York.

The title series stood two wins for the Knicks, two for the
Lakers as play continued in game number five at Madison
Square Garden. With 3:56 left in the first period, the Lakers
had built a 25-15 lead with some of their best play of the entire
season. Reed, who'd been bothered earlier by a sore left knee
and by a jammed shoulder, drove toward the basket. He
swerved awkwardly as he rumbled to the hoop to avoid contact with Chamberlain. The move was not natural, and as he
made it he felt a knife-blade pain in his right hip. A muscle
was torn, and he fell to the floor, convulsing in agony, as
action continued at the other end of the court before play
could be halted.

"It's all over! We've gone so far and it's all over!" Reed recalls thinking as he limped off the floor with the help of trainer Danny Whelan.

New York was forced to go with slender reserve center Nate Bowman and forward Bill Hosket, just 6-foot-7, without Reed for the rest of the half, and Los Angeles forged a 53-40 lead. Despair was the prevalent emotion. Reed meant leadership as well as rebounds and field goals for the Knicks, and he was gone. How could the Lakers possibly be beaten now?

Resourceful Red Holzman, the New York coach, instructed his team during the intermission, "Create havoc." He wanted full-court pressing tactics, accelerated tempo, extra effort at reaching out with hands and knees and elbows to disrupt the Lakers and prevent their taking advantage of Reed's departure.

The final two quarters were marked by both the havoc Holzman urged and by mayhem. The Knicks, urged on by their partisan mob, forced Los Angeles into an eventual 30 turnovers, 10 in the final period alone. With Reed already undergoing the frenzied ministrations of trainer Whelan back in the locker room, the Knicks emerged with a 107-100 victory.

Reed flew, along with his teammates, back to the Forum in Inglewood for game number six. No one thought he could play or that the Knicks could win two in a row without him, winding up the series, but Whelan's heat, ultra-sound, and whirlpool-bath treatments could continue without interruption. As expected, the Lakers won easily as Chamberlain scored 45 points to prolong the series, and Reed was seen to leave the Knicks' bench well before the final buzzer. He rushed to nearby Los Angeles International Airport for a night flight back to New York for further treatment beginning early the next morning, which, it was hoped, might ready him for play in the title-deciding game.

Bulletins were issued almost hourly by the Knicks as game time approached. *Reed felt better. Reed felt worse. Reed thought he could play. Reed feared he couldn't play. Reed was hopeful he could play. Reed grimaced dismally because he could not.*

The teams arrived at Madison Square Garden late that

afternoon and sequestered themselves in their dressing rooms. Treatment continued for Reed as his teammates dressed and began pregame warmups. Fans buzzed with conversation as they filed into the huge new arena built above Pennsylvania Station, but without the usual raucous vitality which marks New York crowds on less tension-filled occasions.

Would Reed play? Would the Knicks, keystone franchise of the original Basketball Association of America of 1946, win the league title for the first time? Would a season of mounting hope end with frustration?

It all boiled up and out, uproariously and viscerally, when Reed hobbled onto the court. The Lakers were pros and did not fold at the surrealism of this epic moment. But the Knicks were reborn with fleetness of foot and sharpness of eye when their captain reported to lead them, and the grandeur of the moment was not wasted as the New York victory came to pass.

"It was all worth it," said Reed after the flashbulbs stopped exploding and the champagne corks popped their last pop. "It was a fun game, even with the pain."

"Willis contested Wilt beautifully," said Dave Stallworth, a member of the Knicks' Minutemen corps of aggressive reserves. "That was the game. We knew that if we contained Chamberlain, we could beat their other four."

Said Reed, beginning to wince even more noticeably as the effects of additional halftime injections of painkillers began to wear off, "I knew I couldn't stop Wilt once he made up his mind to drive. So I tried to block his momentum.

"We all knew we had to play this way. You've got to give it all you have. We don't know if we'll ever get this far again. This is a tough league with a lot of great players. That's why we knew we had to give it everything. There might not be a tomorrow."

/ / /

There was time in the off season, after Reed accepted great honors and a multitude of special awards as Most Valuable Player in the championship series, for his right hip to heal. He was the toast of New York ... a title than which, in our century, there is no toastier. Further glories and riches should have showered upon him, such was his stature in the eyes of his fellow New Yorkers.

Instead, the next three years blurred in alternating hazes of depression and achievement, pain and slow recovery. The hip injury, itself long-healed, stands in the perspective of time as one in a series of agonies which have benched Reed for extended periods, to the point that in the pantheon of all-time great NBA centers he will be remembered for his near-tragic role as a flawed, oft-crippled, inspirational leader of a remarkable team.

His left knee had troubled him all through the championship year. Ice was applied after games to slow the inflammation of tendinitis. Heat was applied before games to help heal it. Sometimes, the pain made going after rebounds absolute agony. Sometimes, there was no relief from the torture through long nights.

These things were known by his teammates and by others in pro basketball. His endurance and patience with himself, in the face of pain, were factors which earned him honor as the league's Most Valuable Player in the glorious championship season.

There was no lessening of problems in 1970–71. He continued to play, but with decreasing effectiveness. New York won the Atlantic Division title, but lost in the Eastern Conference playoff finals to Wes Unseld and Earl Monroe and the Baltimore Bullets, four games to three. Afterward, he agreed to surgery and then, through a difficult and hot summer, he worked hard at rehabilitating himself so that he could return to the Knicks healthy for 1971–72.

"I still have the pain in the left leg, especially when I put heavy pressure on it," said Reed in late August after a session of weight-lifting and jogging at New York Military Academy in Cornwall-on-Hudson, New York, where he operates a camp for boys each summer. "But the pain is a twinge in comparison with the pain I experienced last season. Dr. Patterson [Knicks' orthopedic specialist Dr. Andrew Patterson] had to gather the scar tissues and sew them together. Until that stretches itself out, it will continue to pain. The more I run, the better it should get."

Talking with sportswriter Sam Goldaper of *The New York Times,* he added, "During some of those painful times last season, I made up my mind that I would undergo surgery even if the doctors told me there was only a fifty-fifty chance I would play again. I would have taken that chance, even with less odds. It just didn't make any sense to play any longer at seventy or seventy-five per cent of capacity. I value myself too much as a person and a player to do that."

Concerned that Reed could not, after the surgery, play his usual 45 to 48 minutes a game, the Knicks sought someone during the off season who might spell Reed from time to time in the 1971–72 campaign. They offered a sharp-shooting member of the Minutemen, forward Cazzie Russell, to the Golden State Warriors in exchange for 6-foot-8 veteran Jerry Lucas. An All-Star with Cincinnati and, before that, a three-time All-American from Ohio State, Lucas had played forward most of his pro career, including a season on the West Coast. He was admittedly too small and too slender to play center in the Reed style . . . but he would do. Centers being as scarce as they are, he would *have* to do.

Reed reported to the Knicks' Monmouth College preseason training camp in New Jersey and labored to recover his former usefulness. The marvelous agility and power leaping just wasn't there. On November 11, he limped off the court during a game against Golden State . . . and never returned to the lineup that season. He rested a while, hoping the tendon in his left knee would heal. Then he tried work to get back to playing shape—with no success. On February 5, the Knicks announced he would sit out the remainder of the season in the hope of returning for 1972–73.

In consultations between Dr. Patterson and Dr. Dan O'Donoghue, a nationally regarded specialist who headed the orthopedic department of the University of Oklahoma Medical School, it was agreed that Reed's left leg would be immobilized for six weeks by a walking cast. Afterward, there would be more therapy . . . and, if all went well, a return to peak condition at last.

Lucas's outside shooting, posing unique defensive problems for opposing centers of the Bill Russell mold who preferred to stay deep underneath the basket, and the midseason addition of Monroe from Baltimore gave the Knicks enough strength to finish second in the division and to upset Boston in the Eastern Conference finals. It was anticlimactic, however, for 1971–72 was the season of Wilt Chamberlain and the Lakers.

Los Angeles won 33 in a row in midseason and was championship-bound as assuredly as the Knicks had been in 1969–70. Reed was only a frustrated spectator in May as the Lakers won the title in five games.

Again, after another painful summer, Reed fought back against pain and the tedium of recovery. He shared center time with Lucas in 1972–73 in a season which, for the first time since pre-Russell days, had no clearly dominating, obviously title-destined team.

Boston and Milwaukee were installed hesitantly as championship favorites, but the Knicks upset the Celtics in the Eastern Conference finals, and the Lakers toppled Golden State in the West following the Warriors' upset series win over Milwaukee. Reed was honored, two weeks later, as playoff MVP when the Knicks regained the world title with victory over the Lakers in five games.

If reality could be manipulated and constructed with the tidy symmetry of a novel, Reed's career would have continued following his great comeback with further glory and honor. Having returned from the despair of possible career-ending pain and injury to lead his team back to pre-eminence, he should have been able to go on to greater glory just as fictional heroes do after great plot-point traumas.

Instead, he once more experienced a wrenching descent from the exhaltation of a championship locker-room celebration to self-doubt and misery in a hospital's postsurgery recovery room.

The 1973–74 season had opened with Reed the incumbent at center, Lucas scheduled for relief duty behind him and also for part-time duty at forward, and with a mop-haired, gawky young man from the University of the Pacific in Stockton, California, 6-foot-10 John Gianelli, as a third center to be nurtured slowly for an eventual role as Reed's successor.

In early November, however, Reed was forced out of the game following a scramble for a loose ball against the Lakers at the Forum. Pain was no stranger to him, but this time it was his right knee that agonized, not the left. Examination showed cartilage injury. Rest was prescribed in the hope that, as sometimes happens, the knee would heal itself. He tried to play, briefly, against the Capital Bullets on November 25, but was in too much pain to continue.

For a bookkeeper or a lawyer, the doctors might have suggested rest, a brace, caution, and, "Lay off the Sunday tennis for a couple of years." But Reed is a professional athlete whose career could not be indefinitely suspended. He was needed back and reasonably healthy as quickly as possible.

Thus, on December 12, he arrived at St. Anthony's Hospital in Oklahoma City for another session on the surgical table. Dr. Donoghue was the attending physician again. He removed not only a portion of the ripped cartilage, but also a bone spur at the rear of the knee which had caused Reed intermittent discomfort. "It was actually two operations in one," the patient would later recall.

Reed was familiar, by now, with the recovery procedure. A cast would keep the leg immobile while the tissue healed from the surgery. During immobility, there would be weight gain. The unused muscles of the right leg would shrivel, lose their ability to contract and expand in the sudden bursts of effort that had sent him soaring into the air to pluck off a re-bound or block a shot. The muscles would have to be rebuilt, there would have to be adjustment to playing with a per-manently impaired knee, weight would have to come off his tummy and upper body, and general muscle tone would have to be regained in order for him to resume his role as leader of the Knicks.

"The situation is a lot different this time than before," Reed told New York reporters on January 3 when he returned to Manhattan from convalescence at his parents' home in Ber-nice, Louisiana, for a press conference ironically staged to help promote a new book pictorially detailing his recovery from the tendon surgery and leading to the 1972–73 championship. "The injury this time was defined. There was no guessing this time. The surgery was performed, the cartilage and spur removed. I know what I have to do. I hope to be able to return to the team by March 1."

He left New York again, returning to Louisiana to work at the direction of Doc Harvey, the trainer at Grambling College who had ministered to him during his outstanding under-

Sore-kneed superstar challenges sore-kneed superstar as New York's Willis Reed drives for basket against Capital Bullet's Wes Unseld in 1973–74 Eastern Conference playoffs

graduate career. "It's better for Willis to begin his therapy at Grambling, where he won't be hounded and distracted by a lot of people," said Danny Whelan, the Knicks' trainer.

Periodic progress reports were made in the next two months. The knee was healing, but March 1 came and passed, and Reed was still working himself back to playing condition as the Knicks maintained second place in their division.

The Grambling work had brought enough improvement so that Reed could return to New York. At Pace College gym in New York a week after his too optimistic target date, Reed was interviewed by columnist Jerry Izenberg. There had been a fast-paced hour of shooting all by himself, followed by a torturous hour of quick starts and stops, bends and jumps at the command of physical therapist Joseph Zohar. Finally, huffing and puffing, he sat down with Izenberg to talk about his status and his future.

"Do you think," Izenberg asked, "that the average fan can possibly relate to the pain and the doubts?"

"No," Willis said, "he can't. But I don't think the management can, either. I don't even think you can. It's a lonely, hard thing.

"It's pain, but it's more than that. It's the way you have to drive yourself. You have to push and push and you have to do it.

"Anywhere along the line, you could get discouraged and blow it. But I won't. I won't blow it. I'm doing what I have to do.

"I gave almost all of my life to basketball. That's the dues I paid. It's up to me now to know what I can do and for how much longer I want to do it.

"You read things . . . you hear things. . . . People say I ought to quit. They said that a few years back about me. And then we won. And they didn't say anything for a while.

"I'll do what Joseph over there tells me to do. I'll work as hard as I know I have to work. I'll be back. I want to come back . . . and I will. It's a lonely thing, but I've come too far from Bernice [Louisiana] not to try."

The tantalizing thing, as Reed implied, was the history of the Knicks during the four years since their first world championship. Under the clever coaching of Holzman, the team had started slowly each season, meshing younger players into the team-play style of the club, and then managed to peak just in time for a smash effort in the playoffs. Boston had won the division championship during the two previous regular seasons and would win again in 1973–74, but the Knicks had prevailed twice during the playoffs . . . without Reed the first time, with him the second. The rush for recovery was to get Reed back into action while games remained in the regular season. No matter how hard he might work in the gym or even, finally, in off-day scrimmages with his teammates, only game competition could hone him sufficiently to prepare him for the playoffs and for the attempt to topple Boston once more.

Finally, at Phoenix on March 22, 1974, the hulking man wearing number 19 for the Knicks played for his team once again. It was only for eight minutes and he scored just four points, but it was emotionally a rich occasion.

"It means a lot to our team to see that Willis can be out there for some part of a game," said Bill Bradley with his usual earnest demeanor. "I don't think we look to him any longer to be the top scorer or to play forty-eight minutes, but when he does the things he can do for even part of a game, it makes us much stronger."

Said Reed following a 106-104 New York victory, "I felt all right. I've done a lot of work with weights on both legs and I'm going to continue to do more. I wasn't conscious of any difficulty or worry. The main thing for me was that when a couple of situations arose, I reacted instinctively, without thinking, and jumped or moved the way I was supposed to. I'm not in real shape now, but I will be."

The return was too late to provide the tough preplayoff work Reed needed. He could play for brief periods, but, try as he might, his former intensity was not there. The intimidating effect he had on opponents wasn't there, either.

It took the Knicks seven frantic games to get past Elvin Hayes, Unseld, and the Capital Bullets in the first round of the playoffs. Coach Holzman, getting a surprisingly fine defensive effort by young Gianelli on Hayes, but missing Reed's bulk to counter the bullish Unseld, noted sadly after the sixth game, "I don't think we can count on Willis for any sustained periods of time. He's making some progress, but he's nowhere near where he used to be. I'm afraid we can't look to him for any major contributions."

Holzman's somber prediction proved agonizingly accurate in the next two weeks. Reed could be used only briefly in the conference championship series, and, for the first time in three years, Boston toppled the Knicks handily—four games to one.

It was hoped, later, that Reed might continue his physical therapy and recovery in the coming summer. DeBusschere retired to become general manager of the ABA's New York Nets and Lucas retired to a career in business and entertainment. Bradley had considered a political campaign in New Jersey, thought better of it, but clearly would not remain a professional athlete too much longer. It was up to Willis to provide leadership for a new rebuilding. A summer of therapy and medical examination offered no remedies. In September, reluctantly, he announced his retirement. Not even further surgery would mend him. Willis Reed and the Knicks had come full circle.

/ / /

In 1964, he was little known outside Louisiana or outside the compact universe of the pro basketball executives and scouts. The small, all-black colleges of the South received scant national attention at the time, but far-traveling Red Holzman, chief scout for the New York Knicks, had visited Grambling several times during the past several years to talk to Coach Fred Hobdy and to watch a strong, left-handed youngster named Willis Reed play center.

The Knicks, determined at all cost to begin a climb to respectability, seemed certain to draft number one and were determined to obtain, at last, an outstanding center.

Players at larger schools received greater All-American recognition and a small, quick, aggressive team from UCLA had emerged as number one in the country for the first time, but the nation's more astute fans and certainly everyone in pro basketball regarded three less publicized men as the country's best pro prospects—Reed of Grambling, listed at 6-foot-10 although not quite that big; Lucius Jackson of tiny, integrated Pan American University of Texas, 6-foot-9 and 240; and

awesomely muscular Jim (Bad News) Barnes of Texas Western University of El Paso, 6-foot-8 and 250.

It was vital for competitive success as well as sheer self-
respect that the Knicks choose correctly. The selection of Art
Heyman rather than Nate Thurmond still rankled fans, and
there was also the bitter memory fresh in New Yorkers' minds
of the year (1960) the club selected Cal's Darrall Imhoff first
and permitted the Lakers to pluck a kid from West Virginia
named Jerry West.

Compounding the dilemma was the fact that 1964 was an
Olympic year. The Knicks were among the first teams to hire
a full-time scout and might, in other years, have regarded
Reed or Jackson as "sleepers" whom other teams might not
have discovered. There would be no hiding them, though,
because they were among players invited to try out for the
United States Olympic team in a series of trials held at Singer
Bowl on the grounds of the New York World's Fair. Holzman,
Coach Eddie Donovan, and President Ned Irish would have
an opportunity to see Barnes, Reed, and Jackson play on the
same court at the same time . . . but representatives of every
other pro team would be on hand, too.

The series of games among all-star teams made the Knicks'
choice more difficult, not easier. Barnes and Jackson played
well, but Reed was troubled by a heavy cold and failed to
display the potential Holzman had noted on his trips to Grambling. Barnes and Jackson were elevated several notches on
most pro teams' final draft lists and Reed was demoted to
lesser consideration.

At the close of the trials, Barnes was a unanimous choice for
the United States team as one of the NCAA representatives
along with Walt Hazzard of UCLA, Bill Bradley of Princeton,
and the consensus All-American center, awkward 7-footer
Mel Counts of Oregon State, among others. The National
Association of Intercollegiate Athletics (NAIA) had a much
less powerful voice on the selection committee than did the
NCAA, and only one man from its ranks would be chosen—
Jackson.

A week later, the NBA held its draft. The Knicks chose
Barnes . . . as everyone expected them to do. He was the more
advanced of the trio, having played a stronger collegiate

schedule, and it was felt he could help the Knicks make the greatest immediate improvement. Jackson was big and strong, but might not develop much beyond his senior-year maturity. Reed, the Knicks felt, had the greatest potential, but the club was not prepared to accord itself the luxury of patience.

The draft continued. Detroit went for quick Joe Caldwell of Arizona State. Baltimore, expected to draft Jackson, instead chose slender Gary Bradds of Ohio State. Philadelphia, next in line, grabbed Jackson even though the 76ers already had a fair country center on their roster in a guy named Chamberlain.

The Knicks' staff at the draft meeting played poker face each time another name was called. Reed's subpar performance in the Olympic Trials apparently had fooled several teams' scouts, and there were other teams which bypassed him because they were choosing for position and need rather than for over-all talent. Others were committed to home-town heroes. Eddie Donovan fairly quivered with excitement as the second round of selections opened, therefore, when he proclaimed, "We take Willis Reed of Grambling."

While Barnes, Jackson, Bradley, Hazzard, and other pro draftees headed for Tokyo and the Olympics, Reed prepared himself for the opportunity he'd worked hard to earn ever since he was 13 years old. He agreed to a $14,000 bonus for signing and reported to the Knicks' preseason camp. Early on, he established himself as a remarkable rookie by rapping on Coach Donovan's hotel-room door the first night of training to ask for an NBA rule book. No rookie he'd ever heard of had ever shown that much application, Donovan later recalled.

When the season opened in Madison Square Garden—the old, since-razed historic Madison Square Garden at Forty-ninth Street and Eighth Avenue—Willis Reed was the starting center and Barnes was in the lineup as a forward. They wound up as the Knicks' two leading scorers, having averaged 19.5 and 15.5 points per game, respectively. The Knicks finished last again in the Eastern Division, but they'd improved their record from 22-58 without their two big rookies in 1963–64 to 31-49 with them. True rebuilding had finally begun.

/ / /

There was a three-year period of further growth and transition between the close of Reed's rookie season and the final ascent to the NBA championship four years later. In November 1965, there came a trade engineered by Donovan (elevated to the role of general manager) which brought 6-foot-11 Walt Bellamy to the Knicks for Barnes and two journeymen, Johnny Egan and Johnny Green. Bellamy was as talented as he was inconsistent, but he scored lots of points. Reed coped manfully with the problems of playing forward against smaller, more mobile, men and rewarded the Knicks for their patience with him by earning All-NBA recognition even though he was playing out of his natural position.

There were coaching changes. Reed underwent successful surgery for a bone spur in his right foot. And in December of 1968 came the trade of Bellamy and reserve Howie Komives to Detroit in exchange for heady forward Dave DeBusschere; Reed moved back to center. Elevation of Holzman from scout to coach and the switch of Dick McGuire from coach to Holzman's slot as talent hunter was a final step toward success.

There was trauma in the climb greater than the physical punishment and greater than the disappointments which preceded the championship.

"People think an athlete's life is so glamorous," Reed said in April 1974, looking back at his career in an interview with Kay Gilman of the New York *Daily News.* "It's the only life I've ever known, but there are so many things you have to give up, right from the start. Whatever I do as an athlete comes from my body, and if you want to be good, really good, you have to say 'no' to nights out, to all kinds of things you might like to do. You have to concentrate, put out, be prepared to sacrifice."

One sacrifice, the most painful, perhaps, was his marriage.

"The problem was that it was too soon. I was so young, only twenty-one," Reed said. "If I had waited until I was twenty-six or twenty-seven, maybe we would have been able to make it. But, at twenty-one, I had never been to New York. I went through so many radical changes in my life style. I had to borrow money to get married, and when I was divorced I was making a hundred thousand a year. We had two children in the six years we were married, a son, Karl Vance, who is ten

now, and Veronica Marie, who is eight. Sure I miss my kids. I
see them when I can. I love to do things with them and talk to
them on the phone.

"Sometimes I think that my divorce was one of the worst
things I could have done. I think marriage is very difficult for
a professional athlete. It's the travel, the fact that the men are
famous and idolized—the wives feel left out."

Some day, he said, he hoped to remarry. There is a loneli-
ness in his life which has been more profound because much
of his late career was spent recovering from his series of
injuries.

"I'd like to play two more years if I can," he said, with
unfounded optimism, "and then I'd like to see so many things
in the United States and the world that are worth seeing. I like
to work with kids, to encourage them to make something of
themselves, showing them that if I could do it, they can, too.

"My career has always had first priority, and after I finish
I'd like to stay in basketball in some capacity. But I believe in
fate and predestination. If I had a magic wand I'd touch my
knees and make them healthy, but life isn't that simple. When
I look at other people, I realize how much I have to be
thankful for.

"I had it tough. I had to stand alone from the start. That
made me a strong-willed person—as stubborn as a mule. If I
want something, if it's in my capacity, I will do it. I had a coach
at Grambling who once said to me, 'Always aim for the moon.
If you don't get the moon, you'll catch a star.'"

For Willis Reed, the moon and all the stars were the NBA
championship in 1970 . . . the night he hobbled onto the court
to battle Chamberlain and the Lakers. To have played on a
world-championship team was a fulfillment for him as an
individual. To win a world championship was a vindication for
his management and his teammates. But to perform with such
heroism in New York City with the entire nation looking on in
admiration lifted more than just a man or a franchise . . . it
lifted an entire league and insured him regard, as long as
NBA games are played, as the man who established for all
time the emergence of basketball as a major, national professional sport.

7

THE SENSITIVE EGO WITH THE SENSITIVE TOUCH: ELVIN HAYES

The San Diego Rockets were a team of youngsters in October 1968, and, as young athletes will, they sat sprawled in an insolent manner, in groups of twos and threes, white and black, on the plush lobby furniture of the Caravan Inn in Phoenix. Arizona.

Luggage was stacked by the entryway, waiting for the bus to arrive for a brief ride to Sky Harbor Airport, and the players chattered about their on- and off-court successes, about their plans for the night to come in San Francisco.

Airline stewardesses and hotel employees walked past, now and then, on their way to and from the coffee shop, and vacationing couples and singles walked by, too. The players leered and gossiped, enjoying the morning and the sheer fact of being young, vigorous, athletic, and on the road.

Two older players, cast adrift by their original teams and made available to the Rockets in the expansion draft of the previous season, sat quietly, reading the morning sports pages' accounts of the exhibition loss to the Phoenix Suns the night before. The club was carrying seventeen players, and five would have to be cut before the regular season opened.

Management was committed to building with youth and the veterans were justifiably concerned for their jobs.

One member of the team, tall, black, and muscular, sat uncomfortably on the arm of a sofa, away from the main group of players. He wore a scowl, and a toe tapped nervously. His arms were crossed over his chest in a posture which said clearly to students of body language, "Just leave me alone."

Rookie Elvin Hayes clearly was an unhappy young man, though he had greater reason than anyone on the team to be jolly. His talent was enormous, his potential unlimited. He'd signed a contract calling for well above $100,000 for each of his first three seasons as a pro, a highly lucrative deal for the time. He knew that the Rockets, having won the flip of the coin and having drafted him first in the previous spring's college draft, looked to him as their *great big man* to make a successful franchise out of the losingest team in the league.

Still, he was unhappy. And so he waited along with his teammates, but isolated from them by his smoldering rage, for the ride to the airport and the morning flight to San Francisco.

I was traveling on a preseason scouting assignment for *Sports Illustrated* that week, gathering quotes and observations on Western teams which later would be incorporated in the magazine's annual preseason issue.

Hayes clearly needed *someone* to talk to, and I approached.

"It's terrible," he confided bitterly. "I'm trying to help this team, but the white boys won't pass to me! How can I help if I don't get the ball?"

I mumbled something consoling, *tsk tsk*ing in sympathy. I'd met him when the road trip began, and, despite what I'd been told, found him likable and interesting.

"The man [meaning Coach Jack McMahon] gotta do somethin'," Elvin continued unhappily.

"Elvin," I said, hoping to ease his anxiety at least a little, "I don't know for sure that you're wrong. But I'll tell you this— this team has you, now, so it's got a good center. But it's still not really a team. And, Lord, how it needs a playmaker. Guys aren't passing to you—but guys on this team don't pass much to anybody! That's one of the problems. I don't think black and white has anything to do with it. I think dumb basketball is the problem, not bigotry."

Hayes promised to think about that, pleased that I'd acknowledged his skill as a center. Earlier, he'd said without undue emphasis that he felt he was, even before having played exhibition game number one of his pro career, already fourth best in the league, behind only Bill Russell, Wilt Chamberlain, and Nate Thurmond. The claim had come more as a matter-of-fact statement than as a boast.

My job, among others for the magazine, was to estimate just how accurate Hayes's self-appraisal might be. The measurement would come in San Francisco when, for the first time, he would play against Thurmond.

The morning after the game, I sought out the rookie to get his impressions. The interview took place as we marched through San Francisco International Airport toward the boarding gate for the flight home to San Diego.

"Tell me, Elvin," I asked, "how was it to play against Nate for the first time?"

The rookie didn't break stride, but neither did he reply without taking a moment to consider the correct answer.

"How many points I get?" he said finally, answering a question with a question.

"Eleven," I reminded him, puzzled.

"How many points Nate get?" Hayes continued.

"Twelve."

"How many rebounds I get?"

"Ten."

"How many rebounds Nate get?"

"Sixteen."

"How many shots I block?"

"Eight."

"How many shots Nate block?"

"Two."

Elvin halted his march. He broke into a self-satisfied smile. "Well?" he grinned.

"Well what?" I said.

"Well," he said, resuming his walk to close the discussion, "that tell you how it was to play against Nate."

A brash rookie named Elvin Hayes outmaneuvers and outleaps veteran Nate Thurmond to haul down a rebound in October 1968

This strange catechism was Hayes's way of saying that he felt he'd more than held his own, despite inexperience, against a proven master of center play.

Twin factors in Hayes's early career were well evidenced by the two conversations. On one hand, he felt an injustice was being done him. On the other, he was proud of his own performance and he was insistent that he be credited for it.

Pushed one way and the other in his psyche, Hayes was frequently petulant and moody, a constant problem for Coach McMahon, General Manager Pete Newell, and the club's owner-president, Bob Breitbard. Moderate success followed, in that attendance picked up and the team finished fourth in the Western Division (to earn what remained the club's only playoff appearance until the season of 1974–75), but the price paid by Hayes and everyone else on the team was high. Tempers were short, and there might have been eruptions had the team not been exhilarated at its climb from the cellar.

So sensitive was Hayes to real or imagined slights in his early career that teammates began to laugh at him . . . when he was out of earshot, of course.

"Did you hear about the E?" one player asked another, according to an NBA legend.

"No. What happened now?"

"He went to a Chargers game last Sunday, but left before the first quarter was over."

"Yeh? What happened?"

"The quarterback called the Chargers into a huddle, and Elvin, up in the stands, got really teed off."

"Why?"

"Hell, you know Elvin—he thought they were talking about him!"

/ / /

Victories became harder to come by in Hayes's second season, and Jack McMahon was fired in favor of another veteran professional, Alex Hannum—the same 6-foot-7 ex-hatchet man whose personal stature, physically and morally, had been so instrumental in helping guide Wilt Chamberlain toward all-around team play seven years earlier at San Francisco. The change was made too late in the season for Hannum to do much with a floundering team, but he had high ambitions for his first full season as coach of the Rockets. And Hayes shared those ambitions with him.

That summer, I talked with Elvin for a magazine piece I was writing. His outlook was optimistic almost to the point of euphoria. He felt the worst was over for him, and that team success and personal acclaim nationally were just around the corner.

First, we talked about what he'd accomplished statistically and about the failure of the nation's basketball fans to regard him as a superstar. He recited, without reference to notes, some of the things he'd already done in basketball:

ITEM: In two years as a professional, he'd been the NBA's leading and then fourth highest scorer, the fourth highest and then leading rebounder.

ITEM: In two years as a professional, he twice had been the most durable athlete in the league. He had yet to miss a game. Twice, he had led the league in total minutes played.

ITEM: Before coming to the pros, he'd been voted College Basketball's Player of the Year. Lew Alcindor had been runner-up.

ITEM: Before coming to the pros, he had set NCAA career and/or single-season records for total field goals and total points, and in several other vital categories. That some of these marks have since been broken does not dim the fact that he accomplished more in these statistical categories than any of the hundreds of thousands of collegians who had come before him.

ITEM: Before coming to the pros, he scored 39 points and added 15 rebounds to lead his university to a victory over Alcindor and UCLA which ended a 47-game Bruin winning streak and which was watched by the largest crowd—more than 50,000 at the Houston Astrodome—ever to see a basketball game.

And finally . . .

ITEM: Elvin Hayes, despite all these glittering accomplishments, had failed that spring to get so much as a single third-place vote in balloting among his fellow pros for Most Valuable Player after leading the Rockets in 10 of 12 offensive categories.

"What's wrong?" Hayes asked, particularly unhappy that he

wasn't recognized as one of the most productive players in the league.

He was painfully sincere in his wonder at his lack of recognition. There had been little bravado or bluster in the way he'd tolled off his achievements. Instead, as we talked, I felt the pride of a young man who had, through his talent and through Lord knew how much pain and effort, climbed from the deepest poverty to assured financial security for himself and his family.

At age eight, he had worked the cotton fields around Rayville, Louisiana, adding to a large family's poverty-level income. Within a couple of years, still a boy, he was working from four in the morning until noon, without a break, for four or five dollars a day. And then had come school in the ramshackle, primitive facilities Dixie provided for its country blacks, followed, at the end of dispiriting days, by hours of shooting a stuffed sock or some other makeshift missile through a scrap-metal improvised hoop tacked to a pole or a tree in a dusty, dirt farmyard.

The transition from Eula Britton High School to the University of Houston and then to conservative, WASPish San Diego had not been easy.

As a boy, he spoke little with strangers—especially with the infrequent white strangers—because a speech impediment made him difficult to understand. He was sensitive to ridicule because he mumbled and slurred so badly. But his growth to his eventual 6-foot-9, 235-pound maturity, his quickness, and his over-all ability became well known throughout the basketball underground of the South.

Isaac Morehead knew about Hayes in 1964, and paid a call one day on Guy Lewis, the basketball coach at the University of Houston.

"There's a kid over at Rayville," said Morehead, " and he's got everything to become another Bill Russell."

"If he's that good," Lewis later recalled asking Morehead, "why are you telling me about him?"

"I'd like to have him," said Morehead, who was the coach at all-black Texas Southern University, not far from Houston's campus, "but I can't get him. His coach went to Grambling, two of his sisters worked their way through Southern U. [in

Louisiana]. I don't want him at either place. We've got to play both of them. Anything I can do to help you get him, just call on me."

Responding to Lewis's recruiting, instigated at Morehead's urging, Hayes helped integrate what previously had been an all-white student body at Houston. While the team reached national prominence and Hayes became an All-American, his social adjustment in a hostile environment was slow and painful. It was typical of Hayes's ambition and pride that he majored in, of all things, speech, and, in time, overcame his boyhood impediment.

In his senior season, the pressures and expectations built to far beyond what a youngster with his background should have had to endure.

First came the Astrodome victory over Alcindor and UCLA, perhaps the most publicized college game of all time. Then came the NCAA championships at the Los Angeles Sports Arena in which the Bruins avenged that defeat with maniacal fury, 101-69, in the semifinals before going on to the national championship. Coach John Wooden employed an unorthodox defense in that game, a *diamond-and-one* combination of four men playing zone and the fifth man playing nose-to-nose with Hayes to shut him off from the ball. Hayes grew more and more frustrated as the game moved toward its humiliating conclusion, and the outcome added to Hayes's reputation as a player incapable of rising to stress or showdown situations.

The American Basketball Association had a team in Houston at the time, the Mavericks (later moved to the East Coast as the Carolina Cougars and subsequently relocated in St. Louis). The club boasted throughout Hayes's senior season of the million-dollar offer it would make which, surely, would win the collegiate Player of the Year for the new league. There were home-town pressures on Hayes to join the Mavericks, but he chose, instead, to sign with San Diego and the NBA.

Under Hannum, anticipating his third season as a pro, Hayes was eager that all his past work and past controversy would finally be rewarded with personal glory and with success for the team.

"Alex was a big man himself," Hayes said in our interview

during the off-season of 1970. "He could help me. He gave me more time, taught me different moves, showed me how to play the pivot position. He helped me on my range of shots, my defense . . . the total game. I really respect him. He really makes you want to play. He's been around so long, and he really knows the game. He can put it into your head. Everybody on the team wants to play."

Hannum didn't attempt to change Hayes's style. Hayes continued to roam around the free-throw line offensively, in position to take passes from his teammates, which he usually turned into line-drive jump shots or powerful drives to the basket. Seldom did he give up the ball to a teammate once it came to him. Defensively, in the model of a boyhood idol, Bill Russell, Hayes played deep to block shots and go for defensive rebounds.

Hayes's shooting frequency remained the highest in the league. In fact, by the time the season ended, he'd attempted 2215 shots, 948 of them successful, for a 42.8 per cent accuracy mark which was only mediocre. It wasn't that he was that poor a shooter. On a team which continued to flounder despite the earlier optimism, he felt forced to take shots that were beyond his range or without good balance or floor position.

The one statistical difference from his first two seasons was a slight drop in minutes played—from 3695 and 3665 to 3633. He was as durable and injury-free as ever . . . but Hannum began to bench him, from time to time, for disciplinary reasons.

Against Phoenix in late November, Hayes scored 37 points and played well in a Rockets victory. At Los Angeles the next night, he made only 7 field goals in 22 attempts and had only 8 rebounds. The Lakers were only one point up at halftime, 52-51, but erupted for a healthy lead midway through the third period and Hannum benched Hayes for the remainder of the game.

"Elvin wasn't feeling well at halftime," said the coach after a 130-112 pasting. "From the way he was playing in the third period, I figured I'd better get him out. I'd rather have a team digging and hustling instead of just going through the motions."

Elvin Hayes's job for San Diego Rockets was to score and score and score, and his best weapon was his jump shot from the top of the key . . . against Seattle and over Bob Rule, in this case

Hayes, dour and not anxious to talk, admitted he'd been exhausted after playing the entire first half. But he'd wanted to get back onto the floor. "I felt I could have gone back in there," he said. "Hell, maybe we could have won. We can't win when I'm sitting there. It's a terrible feeling to be sitting on the bench and watch your team get beat by twenty or thirty points."

Hannum managed to get the team up to third in the Pacific Division, but the record was still a losing tally at 40 wins, 42 losses. The rebuilding plan which was to have emphasized youth had failed, and the Rockets still lacked a floor leader.

Owner Breitbard had to suffer not only the agony of watching his team flounder on the floor, but also a series of financial squabbles with the City of San Diego over operation of the International Sports Arena. There were disputes over taxes and shares of parking revenues, and there were claims by the City Council that the Rockets were behind in payments. Attendance averaged a respectable 6000-plus, but the terms of the lease arrangement were so steep Breitbard had difficulty meeting the high expenses of operation while, at the same time, satisfying his obligation to the city. A member of a family which long had been involved in civic and sports boosterism in San Diego, Breitbard felt betrayed by his fellow townsmen and, by midsummer, decided to accept an offer from a group of Houston businessmen rather than continue to fight with his home city's government.

While the negotiations were being conducted, Hannum bailed out. Anxious to rise above the mere coaching level, he accepted the chance to become coach–general manager and president for a San Diego-based business group which had purchased a team in the ABA. He would still be involved with a team called the Rockets . . . but with Denver of the ABA rather than San Diego of the NBA.

A lure for the Houston interests which bought out Breitbard was the prospect of returning Hayes to the city in which he'd first reached stardom. Houston had grown cosmopolitan in the post-NASA era of moon landings and space-station construction, and there was no concern that the black Hayes might not be eagerly accepted as a hero.

As well as Hayes had spoken of Hannum the previous summer, he was bitter now at the coach's departure. "He was one of the lowest, most conceited people I've ever seen," said Hayes later. "He tried to control me like he was the Lord Almighty Himself."

The new coach was Tex Winter, a one-time University of Southern California teammate of both Hannum and Bill Sharman who had gone into college coaching rather than play pro basketball. He'd been successful in the Big Eight at Kansas State, less successful in the Pac-8 at the University of Washington, and had sought the pro post when it was vacated by Hannum . . . although he'd not known the team would be moving on to Texas.

It was a disaster for the team and for Winter. He was not wise to the guiles and ways of the NBA, and he made the typical mistake of a college man coming to the pros—attempting to treat his players like men, rather than like boys. He discovered too late that, often, a college team may include fewer prima donnas and exhibit greater self-discipline than a pro team composed of immature older men used to stardom.

He installed a complex "triple post" offense which the Rockets had difficulty grasping, and he deprived himself of a certainty—Hayes's scoring—by asking him, for the first time in his career, to think first about passing before attempting to shoot.

"Tex just didn't know what he wanted me to do," Hayes later recalled. "He told me to stop shooting completely. I was supposed to become a passer. I could have done more for the team selling peanuts. But as soon as we started losing, he told me to go back to my normal game—and everything started up again."

"Everything" meant squabbling and jealousies within the team as well as a belated decision to scrap the triple post. Attendance was poor, and the team finished a dismal fourth in the Pacific Division, 35 games behind champion Los Angeles, at 34 wins, 48 defeats.

The off season was a time to take stock under a new team president, Ray Patterson, former general manager-president of the Milwaukee Bucks. Some promising young players had come to the team through good drafts conducted by departing General Manager Newell, and the decision was made by Patterson and Winter to trade Hayes and, in effect, start building all over again.

This was not surprising in itself. The shock came when the deal was announced—Hayes would go to the Baltimore Bullets in exchange for 6-foot-6 forward Jack Marin, and he would become a forward because the Bullets already had an outstanding center in Wes Unseld.

Hayes was not just surprised, he was amazed—because Unseld had long been a special rival. An All-American at Louisville University during Hayes's days at Houston, Unseld was the number two man in the draft Hayes's senior year, and he had been both Rookie of the Year and Most Valuable Player, leading the Bullets to the Eastern Conference championship his first season as a pro. Hayes had outplayed Unseld each time their teams had met that season and his over-all statistics were superior, but Unseld had been acclaimed as a great new influence on pro basketball . . . and Hayes had been dismissed as a trouble-maker.

While Hayes was moody and difficult, Unseld was self-assured and confident. He was the younger brother of a former college star, George Unseld of Kansas, and he'd been regarded as the best high-school player in Kentucky while an undergraduate at Seneca High of Louisville. He had benefited from first-rate coaching at all stages of his career, including hours of one-on-one work with his brother, and he'd learned well to use his 6-foot-7, 240-pound bulk to box out rival rebounders in the battling under the backboards. His special forte was his ability to turn defensive rebounds into fast-break field-goal opportunities for his team. He had the knack of spotting teammates' positions on the floor even before leaping for an opponent's missed shot. Often, he'd make his outlet pass to start the break even before he returned to the floor.

"The Bullets play on a fifty-foot court," people in the NBA used to say, meaning that Unseld's rebounding and passing permitted his team to get frequent, deep offensive penetration well before opponents could race back to defend.

With Unseld, the Bullets were consistent winners for the first time. But they were not good enough, Coach Gene Shue concluded, to become world champions. Something more would be needed, and he'd concluded Hayes could be that *more*.

By December 1972, Shue's belief that Hayes and Unseld might work well together had proven more than justified. There were no eruptions of ego or conflicting ambitions . . . while, at Houston, Winter had still so poorly adjusted to pro ball he was discharged in favor of a well-traveled veteran backcourt star, Johnny Egan.

With Hayes, Baltimore became one of the NBA's élite teams. "There's been no problem between me and Elvin or Elvin and the players," said Shue. "Elvin has been a tremendously hard worker for us, his attitude has been terrific, and, most important, he has given us the potential to be an excellent team.

"I felt we had just about reached our full potential as a team last season, but we were still backsliding. We were losing more than we were winning. Now, with Elvin on our side, we've turned things around for the first time in three years and I know we haven't reached our full potential.

"Elvin has given us his strengths, not his weaknesses. He has helped us primarily with his defense and his rebounding. These are the two areas I've always considered the most important in building a winning team, and this is where he has helped us the most. For the first time since I've been coaching, we have an outstanding shot-blocker who can intimidate the opposition.

"We know Elvin is a great scorer. But we haven't pressured him to score a lot of points. He doesn't have to carry the scoring load for us like he did in Houston. This year, he has played under more control than ever before. He is looking for the good percentage shot and fitting into the team concept of play."

Said one of Hayes's teammates, clever guard Archie Clark, "We're much, much stronger than last year, no doubt, with the addition of Elvin. Elvin gives us rebounding, he gives us shot-blocking, he gives us scoring, plus he gives us flexibility with Wesley. We got two centers now. We can run two different types of center games at teams."

Early in January, the Bullets came to Los Angeles for the

first time that season. While Elvin showered after a brilliant 32-point, 17-rebound performance in a 112-104 victory over the Lakers, I talked with Shue about his daring Hayes-Unseld experiment and about Hayes's career-long reputation for creating problems.

"Hard to coach?" laughed Shue. "Hell, no He's been a real gem. Without him this season, we would be struggling to be anyplace. Elvin has unusual ability . . . ability that can help you win. He has been a really hard worker and he's teamed extremely well with Wes Unseld and I couldn't be more pleased with him."

"What about Elvin demanding to have the ball all the time?" I asked.

"I *want* Elvin to shoot," Shue countered. "We run our plays for Elvin and we want him to shoot. But defense is still our strong point. I'm a defensive-minded coach. Defense wins."

Moments later, no longer the scared and angry 22-year-old whom I'd first met at San Diego but, rather, a self-satisfied and self-assured 28-year-old young veteran, Hayes was eager to talk about his new happiness.

"It's all a matter of pressure," he said. "For the past four years, I was living a nightmare. I was always swallowing some pills to calm my nerves. I couldn't sleep. It was a real bad scene.

"It didn't really matter what I did. Somehow I always got the blame. I led the league in scoring my rookie year, but then I heard complaints that I shot too much. The next year, I led the league in rebounding, but they found fault with my defense or something else. It didn't matter. As long as we were losing, they had to look for *somebody* to blame and it usually wound up being me. It got to the point where I'd try to get lost in the crowd. I was losing my confidence. I figured if I'd hide myself on the court, maybe they'd leave me alone. But I found out there's no escape when you're losing.

"The big thing," he continued, "is that when I came to Baltimore people didn't prejudge me. The coach, the players, and the reporters didn't go by past opinions. They got to know me on a personal basis and judged for themselves. Playing for the Bullets has given me peace of mind again. I know if I make a mistake, the coach isn't going to scream at

Washington Bullets

Wes Unseld, fall of 1973

Washington Bullets

Elvin Hayes, fall of 1973

me. And, when we lose, the coach doesn't come in and start knocking over lockers. He tries to explain what went wrong and reminds us that we can get even by winning the next one."

/ / /

Indeed, the Bullets did much better than just get even. They won the Central Division title by six games, finishing with 52 wins against only 30 losses. It was by far the best record ever for one of Elvin's teams, even though his minutes-played figure was the lowest of his career at 3347 and even though he took only 1607 shots compared to his career high of 2215 the year he played under Hannum. He averaged 21.7 points per game—his career low—but was honored with selection to the All-NBA second team as a forward.

There were even aspirations for a world championship because no team had dominated the league the way, in successive seasons, Milwaukee, New York, and Los Angeles had done. It was too great a dream to dream so soon. New York, regaining the services of Willis Reed, peaked after a season of injuries and rebuilding and eliminated the Bullets in five games in the Eastern Conference playoff semifinals.

Hayes went home to Houston satisfied he'd had his finest season as a pro . . . and eager for better things to come. There was good news, bad news, and then good news ahead of him—to be followed by an emotional and spiritual rebirth which not even Hayes is able fully to explain.

First Shue announced that he was leaving Baltimore to become coach of the weakest team in NBA history, the Philadelphia 76ers, winners of only 9 of 82 games in 1972–73. It would be a new challenge for him, and presumably his contract would be more lucrative than his situation with the Bullets. Good news, however, was the completion of a gorgeous new home court for the Bullets—the Capital Centre at Landover, Maryland, about halfway between the cities of Baltimore and Washington, D.C. Additional pleasant news was the selection by Bullets owner Abe Pollin of veteran professional player and coach K. C. Jones, the ex-Boston Celtic, as Shue's successor.

There were brief problems of adjustment between a new coach and his team, but Hayes was primed for even greater team and individual success when the 1973–74 season opened. He seemed even more open and more content with himself than he had been during 1972–73 and, as the new season got underway, he revealed a profound personal reformation.

"I received a prophecy," he said with fervor. "The voice of God reached me and led me to the Church of Holiness."

He explained, "One day I was cutting the lawn and I got a strong feeling that I should to to church. Now, I used to go every Sunday with my wife, Erna Beth, before we were married. But that was just to be cool, to try and get in with her. I used to laugh at all that jumping and shouting. But, the following Sunday, we took the kids and went to the church in Houston that Erna's family goes to."

After the services, Hayes recalled, "A man said, 'Elvin Hayes, come here. The Lord loves you. The Lord knows you.'"

This was Elder J. L. Parker, Hayes explained. "He told me how I grew up in Louisiana, claimed how I came to Houston, how I went to San Diego, and how I came back to Houston and up to Baltimore. This was information that only I knew, that had not been printed. The man said he had had the message for me for a year, but didn't know how to get through to me."

Hayes explained what his new beliefs meant to him, how they had given him new peace of mind after earlier explorations of the Baptist, Methodist, and Catholic faiths, and how he had found Jesus and surrendered his will to Him.

"I just praise God and thank Him for what He has done to me, how He can make you a new creature. I know He's real because He lives in me. Some will say I'm a religious fanatic. I'll follow Jesus. What are Redskin fans or Bullet fans? 'Fan' comes from the word 'fanatic.' I'll be a religious fanatic. I love the Lord.

"It means a great deal. You get frustrated because you have no peace of mind. Then you get angry on the court and it costs you fifty dollars for a technical foul. Then you lose your concentration. Now I don't have a wandering mind. Jesus is victory. You never lose when you have Him. I didn't find Jesus earlier because I wasn't ready. God will let a man wander through life seeking worldly joys. I'd gotten to where I wanted to be, but I still had no happiness and no joy."

The full acceptance of the Pentacostal sect came after the meeting with Elder Parker. "The pastor wouldn't tell me how I was to be of service, so I began to seek the Lord, to study the Bible, to let Him guide my steps. All the pressures that were bothering me have been lifted away by Him and I am at peace.

"Playing basketball is the way the Lord is using me now. If He didn't want me in professional ball, He would have called me away from it. The day He does this, I'll go with joy in my heart. I can serve as an example for those sinners who can relate to basketball players. And that goes for my teammates, too."

Throughout his career, within the tight community of a basketball team, Hayes—like most athletes—had peppered his speech with vulgarisms, profanities, and obscenities. He was neither more nor less coarse in his speech, within the team, than most players. Following his adoption of the Church of Holiness teachings in so strong a way, however, he spoke only with the purity of a preacher. "The ballplayers didn't think I could change so drastically in such a short time," he laughed, "but I did."

Said one unnamed player to magazine writer Charley Rosen, "Elvin is a great guy, and the first time you hear his Jesus rap it's interesting. But it wears thin after a while. We all respect Elvin's faith. I mean, he really is happy and all mellowed out. He's a better person now. But I don't want to be hearing about it for the rest of the season. Sometimes he's really weird—he sits in the locker room before a game all tranced out with his Bible."

The Washington *Post*'s Mark Asher, whose October story had been a first national revelation of Hayes's new faith, recalled, "On plane trips, Hayes sits alone while his teammates play cards and talk about such worldly joys as women. 'Just wishing, and looking and longing for that,'" Asher quoted Hayes as saying, "'you've committed adultery. It's as much of a sin as the act.'"

By midseason, Hayes had demonstrated fully with his performances that his October revelation of enlightenment and tranquillity was heartfelt. He was one of the most effective players in the entire league with his rebounding and shooting and with his defense, and he helped Baltimore take comfortable command of the Central Division even though Unseld was frequently out of the lineup because of arthritis and inflammation of his left knee. It had to be drained periodically of fluid caused by the scraping of bone against bone.

The Bullets won their division by a breezing 12 games with a 47-35 record and Hayes recorded the best statistics of an already gaudy career. He led the league in both offensive and defensive rebounding (the categories were separated officially for the first time) as well as in minutes played (3602). A 32-rebound effort against Atlanta in November was the individual season high, and he'd punctuated that night with 43 points as well, his personal game high as a pro.

Unseld's hobbling gait was too much to overcome in the playoffs. Although Hayes averaged 25.9 points and 15.8 rebounds per game, the Bullets were eliminated by New York in another furiously played seven-game series, themselves to be eliminated later by Boston.

/ / /

The 1974–75 season perpetuated the pattern. The Bullets won 60 games during the season, equaled in the NBA only by Boston, and were considered co-favorites with the Celtics for the NBA title as the playoffs began. Hayes was magnificent and Unseld his usual reliable rebounding force as Washington eliminated aggressive young Bob McAdoo and the Buffalo Braves. Hayes was again magnificent, and Unseld outstanding, when the Bullets next eliminated Boston in a stirring Eastern Conference title series.

It was considered a forgone conclusion that Washington would be too powerful for the surprising Western champions, the Golden State Warriors. Hayes's final transformation from storm center to acclaimed hero seemed to be imminent.

Hayes's newfound religious faith was tested fully, however, in the next week.

First, a vital ingredient in Washington's brilliant season had been number 3 guard James Jones, signed the previous fall as a free agent following a fine, if little publicized, career in the American Basketball Association. Jones was injured in the Boston series, requiring immediate knee surgery, and the Bullets were deprived of his shot-making and clever court generalship in the title series. Golden State, unable to match the individual skills of the Bullets' starting guards, Kevin Porter and Phil Chenier, shuttled five fresh men constantly and gained unexpected advantage.

Scheduling was a factor, too. Normally, a title series begins with two games on the home court of the team which recorded the superior regular season record. In 1975, however, scheduling demands on the league by the Columbia Broadcasting System for national television forced a change: Game No. 1 would be played at the Capital Centre, but Games Nos. 2 and 3 on the West Coast, so that Game No. 4 could be played on a Sunday at a convenient time back in Maryland. When the Warriors upset Washington in Game No. 1 and then returned to their home city for games Nos. 2 and 3, the psychology of playoff basketball was altered. Take nothing away from the Golden State team—it was inspired and relentless. But the scheduling and home-court advantage did become significant factors.

One win . . . another win . . . another . . . and finally, coming from behind as had become their playoffs hallmark, the Warriors upset Washington for the fourth straight time on Sunday, May 25, to culminate an amazing season and to plunge the Bullets into despair yet another time.

But for Hayes there was a difference. In other years, losing critical and championship games, he had always been looked at later as a personal failure. If his teams had lost, he had always taken the blame. But in 1975, Hayes's maturity and skills were recognized. He did not have a good title series, but no member of his team had been outstanding, either, and it was rather acclaim for Golden State's miracle which concluded the NBA season than ridicule or humiliation for the Big E.

It was a subtle difference, but a vindication, and Elvin could at least return home to Houston after that fourth consecutive upset defeat as a man at peace with himself and with his God.

8

THE YOUNG LIONS:
DAVE COWENS, BOB MCADOO,
BOB LANIER, AND ELMORE SMITH

For the first time since December 1956, no one wore number 6 on his uniform. For the first time since 1956, the Boston Celtics weren't winning. And Arnold (Red) Auerbach was chewing fitfully and fretfully on the frayed butts of his cigars—not lighting them with elegance in the fourth periods of games to celebrate victories. He was a general manager with a problem: how to win without Bill Russell . . . or how to find someone who could do at least some of the things number 6, the all-time all-pro, had done for his team for thirteen glorious seasons.

The answer would be found through scouting, a practice Auerbach had disdained earlier in his years as general manager-coach. When only eight NBA teams existed, a few phone calls in February, March, and April to some of his buddies and ex-players around the country had provided all the information he needed. If he made a mistake—which hadn't happened often—his turn came up again soon enough to offer opportunity to draft again.

Now, with more teams added to the league each season,

scouting had become more and more important to the Celtics and to every other team.

Auerbach spent hours and hours watching college games, sifting information, gathering advice.

He listened with intense interest, therefore, one day in early 1970 when Russell, in town on one of his frequent national speaking trips, paid a call. "I wanna tell you about a college player who will make a helluva pro," Russell is said to have told Auerbach in a conversation which has since become part of pro basketball folklore.

"Who?" asked Auerbach eagerly.

"A guy named Cowens, from Florida State," replied Russell in his clipped, self-assured, bantering way.

"When did you see him play?" asked Auerbach.

"I didn't," said Russell, his calm unruffled despite the surprising admission.

"Then how the hell can you say that?" asked Auerbach, his notorious choler rising at the suspicion Russell was playing games with him.

"I looked into his eyes," smirked Russell, oblivious to the flush of anger creeping up the back of Auerbach's neck. "I could see that he had it." And then came the Russell cackle-laugh.

From any other man, the comment might have been weighed as nonsense. But Russell, more than any other athlete in history, had demonstrated the value of mental toughness . . . of a private demand for excellence . . . of a single-minded determination to meet a personal standard. He had sensed a similar quality, he said, in the youngster from Florida.

Cowens was a shade over 6-foot-8 rather than the 6-foot-10 or bigger professional centers were supposed to be, and he was pale-skinned and red-haired rather than black and Afroed as were most star big men. That didn't matter to Russell. He had been, it should be remembered, the first man to insist that performance ought to be the only criterion for a basketball player's evaluation.

"When I first scouted Dave at Florida State," Auerbach later recalled, having responded to Russell's urging that he investigate the only moderately publicized player, "I didn't have any doubts about his future as a pro. But my original estimate was that he'd probably have to be a forward and a part-time center. What changed my mind was his strength and the way he jumped at training camp. Then there was his attitude. You could see that nobody was going to tell this kid he couldn't do something if he wanted to do it, and Cowens obviously wanted to play center.

"However, just to make sure, Tommy Heinsohn [the ex-Celtic who succeeded Russell as coach] and I decided to go back to Russell for a second opinion. 'Forget his height and play him right where he is,' Russell said. 'You won't be sorry, because nobody is going to intimidate this kid. He may need a little time to get ready, but he'll do the job for you.'"

The Celtics had plummeted from world-championship stature in the 1968–69 season under player-coach Russell to sixth in the Eastern Division in 1969–70—26 games behind the eventual new world champion, New York. Likable-but-awkward Henry Finkel, purchased from San Diego, was a 7-footer, but not a starting-caliber NBA center, and the Celtics, in humiliation, finished with the fourth poorest record in the NBA, only 34 wins compared to 48 defeats. The team failed to reach the playoffs for the first time in 20 years.

Detroit had the poorest record in the Eastern Division and had won the traditional coin flip to determine which team would pick first in the annual draft. The Pistons, never having made the playoffs at all and perpetually rebuilding, chose the consensus best available college center—hulking Bob Lanier of little St. Bonaventure in upstate New York, 6-foot-11 tall and weighing nearly 300 pounds.

Pete Maravich had set innumerable NCAA records for game-, season-, and career-scoring playing under his father, Press, at LSU. He would sell oodles of tickets for whichever NBA club might draft him, but, unlike Lanier, he didn't have the potential to turn a losing team into a winner immediately. San Diego, last in the West and fighting deep financial problems in a feud with the city government over use of its arena, bypassed the expensive Maravich and, instead, drafted a tough 6-foot-7 rebounder from Michigan, Rudy Tomjanovich. Atlanta, having traded for San Francisco's draft spot and eager to land a nonblack potential star to help ticket sales, was willing to gamble $2 million on Pistol Pete.

Then it was Auerbach's turn, the first time in more than a decade he'd had the opportunity to make a choice so early in the proceedings. He announced eagerly, "We pick Cowens of Florida State."

Originally from Newport, Kentucky, a once-notorious honky-tonk town directly across the Ohio River from Cincinnati, Cowens had been a late-bloomer physically. His spurt from 6-footer to 6-foot-5 and then 6-foot-8 had come in his junior and senior seasons. Basketball's fabulous *baron*, Coach Adolph Rupp of the University of Kentucky, had exhibited little interest in him even though he'd helped Newport Catholic High School into the state tournament. Coach Hugh Durham of Florida State, on the other hand, felt Cowens could help him in his efforts at making FSU a national power.

The big redhead became a starter as a sophomore even though he was on the small side for collegiate centers, and when he remained the only white starter on an otherwise all-black team in his senior season, the Seminoles became known, in a rude bit of basketball humor, as "The Busted Flush."

Greater publicity would certainly have come if Florida State had not been ineligible for the NCAA tournament because of alleged recruiting infractions. Jacksonville State, with 7-foot-2 Artis Gilmore its star, was the great nationally regarded power in the Southeast and went all the way to the NCAA finals before losing to UCLA.

Cowens burst into the NBA like a thunderclap. In his first few games, he averaged better than 16 rebounds and the Celtics began to regain the swagger and pride that had been their tradition for so long. At the end of the campaign, Cowens was voted co-Rookie of the Year along with Portland's Geoff Petrie. He'd finished seventh in the league in rebounding, and the Celtics climbed to third in the Atlantic Division with a 44-38 record.

A year later, Cowens was recognized as a full-fledged star. Boston regained eminence among NBA teams after only two non-Russell seasons, a rebuilding process which had seemed, prior to the Russell-inspired draft, a project which might take years.

Cowens played with an intensity and reckless abandon that was unprecedented for a center. Often, he not only started fast breaks with quick outlet passes, he also finished them with slam dunk layups which left his rival centers panting in slow-footed frustration back near mid-court. He ranged all over the floor and, like his 6-foot-5 teammate, John Havlicek, he never seemed to tire. "He plays like a 6-foot-8 Havlicek," Heinsohn, for one, was quick to note.

By his third season, moving in what seemed constantly his highest gear, Cowens could look back and admit, "I feel less talented than a lot of the guys I play against and I know that most of them are a lot taller. But I can run the hundred-yard dash with anyone in the league. To be effective, I've got to use my speed all the time. I've got to force the bigger guys out of their usual patterns and into mine by making them afraid I'll run away from them and score easy baskets. They seem very conscious of my speed now. They're chasing me harder all the time. I started running because I didn't want them to embarrass me, and now they're running so *I* won't embarrass *them*.

"It's the same with my aggressiveness. It's the only way I can play, because, if I don't fight for the positions I want, the big

Dave Cowens dives into floor head first after collision with New York's Jerry Lucas . . . a price he pays for his recklessly abandoned style of play

guys will eat me up. It's absolutely necessary that I box out on every play, even if it means I might not have a chance for the rebound. By keeping my man off the boards, I know I've increased the odds that one of our other guys will get the ball.

"The times I go *really hard* after the ball are when I know we *must* have it. It's my job to get it then. I don't worry about injuries. I'm the one going a little bit nutty out there. I don't get hit because I'm doing the hitting."

The acclaim grew: Cowens, with his all-court play, was establishing a precedent for future centers the way Russell, in his era, had done. He was more offensive-minded than Russell, but his essential role, the theory notwithstanding, was the same as his predecessor's: defense to help force the inaccurate shot, defensive rebounding to turn the missed shot into a Boston possession, the quick outlet pass to generate the fast break, and the follow-up on the offensive boards to turn a teammate's inaccuracy into a second-effort field goal.

Tactics were different, but the strategies similar. Playing with Russell behind them, the Celtics had utilized a pressuring, harrassing defense funneling opponents into the middle where Russell could intimidate them and block their shots. Playing with Cowens, the Celtics relied even more greatly on quickness and ball-hawking, still man-to-man, but forced opponents to the outside and toward mid-court in traditional fashion because Cowens was not the shot-blocker Russell had been.

Cowens was voted the NBA's Most Valuable Player for 1972–73 and the Celtics won more games than ever before in their gaudy history—68. With only 14 losses, they achieved the best record in the league and were favorites to win the playoffs. The indestructible Havlicek injured his right shoulder early in the Eastern Conference title series against New York, however, and the loss of his fire power was too great a handicap to overcome. The Knicks won in seven games, then continued on to the NBA championship with victory over Los Angeles.

The Celtics' record in 1973–74 wasn't as good during the regular season, only 56-26 in an improved league compared to 59 wins put together by Milwaukee. Cowens, showing the first signs of mortality, was rested more frequently and actually missed two games in March because calcification had developed in his left knee, apparently the aftermath of a collision and a deep bruise he'd sustained in November.

The playoffs opened, for the first time in memory, without a clear favorite. Milwaukee had Kareem Abdul-Jabbar and had the league's best record . . . but had lost its quickest guard, Lucius Allen, because of a freak injury late in the campaign which required surgery to repair a savagely torn knee. New York was to get Willis Reed back into action after a season of convalescence from knee surgery. Baltimore was coming, too, and Wes Unseld was supposed to be healthy. Los Angeles had won its division title in the late going, Elmore Smith having replaced Wilt Chamberlain. Chicago and Detroit had finished close behind Milwaukee in the Midwest. And young Buffalo, led by sensational sophomore pro Bob McAdoo, had closed with a rush, too.

The Celtics? They'd flopped in the playoffs the year before. Their razzle-dazzle, full-court-press game was effective for the regular season, but teams could adjust to them easily enough in a seven-game playoff series. And didn't New York have a playoff hex on Boston, anyway?

In six fierce games, however, the Celtics blitzed Buffalo. McAdoo, the 6-foot-10 youngster from North Carolina with the dazzling moves and the quick jump shot, averaged 31.7 points per game, but Boston's pressure and cohesive, playoff-wise team coordination were overwhelming.

Reed's recuperation hadn't peaked as soon as Knicks' loyalists had prayed, and Cowens' quickness and strength all but humiliated young John Gianelli. Reed and Jerry Lucas filled in at center at times, but Boston was on the rampage now and eliminated New York, four games to one, to earn the championship round for the first time since Russell's retirement.

The opposition was Milwaukee and Abdul-Jabbar. And the Bucks, with the better over-all season record, would have the home-court advantage should the series go as many as seven games.

It wasn't elegant. There were few moments of soaring emotion or great drama in the tradition of playoff series of the past. No player rose haltingly from the bench with a crippling injury to lead his team to glory as Reed had done in 1970, and no player performed miraculously to dispel accusations of cowardice or selfishness as Chamberlain had done in 1972. Instead, it was just damned good, exciting, basic basketball.

Milwaukee went to its strength. Struggling to bring the ball upcourt against the Boston pressure, Milwaukee fed Abdul-Jabbar and looked for him to maneuver against the shorter, scrambling Cowens. Boston, smaller on the average than the Bucks, used its quickness and emotion to harrass the dribbler and minimize the time Abdul-Jabbar would have to maneuver for his shot for fear of violating the 24-second rule.

A 15-foot hook shot, under extreme pressure, by Abdul-Jabbar with four seconds left in a second overtime period prolonged the series to seven games. It was the closest the series came to heroic stature, but even then it was a game of scrambling and scratching. Cowens had bid to give the Celtics the title in six games with an injury-risking diving scramble for a steal against the great Oscar Robertson at the close of regulation time, but fouled out late in the second extra period.

And the seventh game, in the inexplicable pattern of essentially one-sided final-title games, was a Boston runaway even though the venue was Milwaukee. Cowens, pushing with his elbows and belly and thighs, using his hands aggressively, swarmed all over Abdul-Jabbar from start to final buzzer. His teammates helped by collapsing inward on the great Milwaukee superstar, crowding him from all sides to prevent him from swinging loose for his unblockable skyhook. He managed only three field-goal attempts in an 18-minute mid-game span, none successful, and Boston regained the league title with a 102-87 romp. Cowens scored 28 points and had 14 rebounds in the title game . . . and led the Celtics, too, afterward in width of grin and delight in victory.

"The other guys never got the ball to Kareem," muttered disappointed Larry Costello, the Milwaukee coach. "The Celtics were fronting him and double-teaming him with a sag. Boston's defense beat us. Their team concept of pressure was more than we could handle. With all the adjustments we tried, we just couldn't cope with it. Boston is a great team with no weaknesses. At least I haven't been able to find any."

A Boston dressing room after a championship-series victory is a frightening place. Scores of reporters and cameramen

Muscling for position, red-headed Dave Cowens confronts Milwaukee's Kareem Abdul-Jabbar during 1973–74 title series. Cowens, outsized by Abdul-Jabbar, neutralized Milwaukee's superstar as one key to Boston's return to NBA championship

crowd into a room built to accommodate a fifth as many people, and pandemonium assails the eardrums in a brain-numbing way. Jammed elbow to elbow, people struggle to get close enough to players to record their responses to generally inane questions, and reason gives way to boisterous gibberish.

In the midst of this writhing mass of humanity in Milwaukee on May 14, 1974, was Red Auerbach, more puffy-jowled and gray-haired than in the Boston victory-celebration scene of five years earlier, but puffing sensuously on his victory cigar in just the way he had in 1969. He shouted for the benefit of anyone with room enough to record his gloating: "This club had desire, desire, desire . . . and the old Celtic pride!"

Tossing the coach into a shower, fully dressed, after title victories is a Celtics tradition suspended during Russell's tenure as boss. Such tomfoolery was too immature and too trivial for such a man. Coach Heinsohn, however, had no such qualms. He'd been shoved into the shower by his players moments before the dressing room was invaded by reporters, and now, dripping wet, his hair matted and spewing water as he turned this way and that, he was eager to express vindication for his and Auerbach's gamble of 1970.

"We came in for a lot of criticism," Heinsohn blurted, "when we drafted Cowens and put him at center. People said we couldn't win a title with a man as small as Dave at center. It took a few years to shut up a lot of so-called experts, but we did it."

Havlicek, narrowly the winner of the series' Most Valuable Player voting over Cowens, put the victory in further perspective: "During the early years of my career with Boston, we looked to Bill Russell for the leadership. But this is the new Celtics and it's our first title. Now the guys all look to me with respect for that leadership. And that makes this the most satisfying title of all."

/ / /

As an individual, Cowens is fascinating. An NBA championship final is the ultimate in sophistication, what with national television and all, but Cowens retains the boyish modesty of his Kentucky boyhood. A bachelor, he lives a spartan personal life, renting a one-room converted bath-house in Weston, Massachusetts, during the season and enjoying quiet, introspective hobbies such as stereo music and auto mechanics. He dresses in a curiously bucolic hodgepodge of outdated jackets and lumberjack plaid shirts, a vast gulf separating him from the fashion consciousness of most of his fellow pros. Cowens has even been known to wear old-fashioned suspenders, of all things! When the season ends, he flees for the quiet of his boyhood roots.

As a force in pro basketball, Cowens is something else. He is the leader of a new generation of pro centers, men who came to the sport in this decade and who have supplanted the men of the 1960s as leaders among whom championships are decided. Abdul-Jabbar is pre-eminent, destined to remain so indefinitely, but his stature was already international when he came to the league and he is the link to the Russell–Chamberlain glory years as much as he is a contemporary figure.

Boston's championship victory, made possible by Cowens' energetic and selfless play, marked a new era for basketball. Yet it was in his development and emergence that this was so, not in the way he played.

Once Russell had established a pattern for modern centers with his shot-blocking and rebounding, pro basketball began to climb in national significance. The emergence of Willis Reed and the New York Knicks as champions in the nation's communications center finalized the sport's growth. NBA games became a fixture and a staple of network television sportscasting, and even the most remote and rural sections of America had the opportunity to see Russell, Chamberlain, Thurmond, Abdul-Jabbar, Reed, and their opponents several times each month.

Young coaches could watch what Russell and the others did, and they could incorporate the pro game's philosophies into what they taught. More important, tall young men ambitious to earn college educations and professional riches could see for themselves what Russell did for the Celtics. They could pattern themselves after him while they were still youngsters playing pickup games on their neighborhood schoolyards. By the time they reached high-school competition, they were far more savvy in the dynamics of fast-break basketball than youngsters of the pretelevision, pre-Russell era had been.

Where once there were style differences in basketball as it

was played in the East, Midwest, South, and Far West, now a national philosophy was emerging. If a team had a Russell-style center on its side, it probably played professional-style ball.

In the case of Bob Lanier, drafted by the Detroit Pistons as the number-one player the year the Celtics drafted Cowens, the link with Russell was even more direct and specific than the impersonal watching of a game on a home television screen in Buffalo, New York.

The Pistons sought out Russell in the 1972 off season and asked that he come to their training camp in the fall to serve for a time as Lanier's personal tutor. There was little wrong with his soft, left-handed jump shot or his inside moves, but he was not the defender or rebounder that a man 6-foot-11 and weighing 275 pounds ought to be. He had been regarded as lethargic and moody, and despite his potential for stardom, he was noted primarily among basketball followers as the owner of perhaps the largest pair of feet ever shod in sneakers. "Bob Lanier doesn't have his shoes shined," giggled Lynn Shackelford, the ex-UCLA All-American who had turned to a career in broadcasting, "he takes them to a car wash!"

Lanier responded to Russell with a versatility and concentration he'd never shown before. "I'm all for becoming a better all-around player," he said. "One hates to hear that he's good only at *this,* but bad at something else."

His development had come slowly because of his immense bulk and because, as big as he was, he'd recovered slowly from right-knee surgery, which ended his college career two games short of an NCAA championship opportunity. He had tripped over a Villanova player in the NCAA regionals and been rushed to a hospital for surgery. He was still recovering from the operation when UCLA won another of its string of national titles a week later, and he was still in his hospital bed two weeks after that when he was drafted by the Pistons and signed to a five-year contract calling for $1.3 million.

During the summer of physical therapy to help rebuild his knee, Lanier manfully fought to keep bulk down. "I was two ninety-four at the end of my sophomore year," he told columnist Leonard Lewin of the New York *Post* the day he reported to the Pistons' Ann Arbor, Michigan, training camp in September of 1970. "Once, I got down to two sixty-four. But I felt really weak at that weight. My weight is good now. I'm two seventy-four. I finished college ball at two seventy-two, so that's not bad."

A compulsive nibbler, Lanier claimed he ate only one meal a day. But he admitted to frequent snacks. Urged to get below 270, he resorted to diet pills. His weight fell somewhat, but his stamina fell even more markedly. He complained of being woozy and he tired quickly, and his rookie-year playing time was limited to less than 30 minutes per game. His shooting grades were high, his other grades mediocre. Concern for his knee and fear that he might reinjure himself added to his uncertainty and failure to perform to his own and the Pistons' expectations.

Lanier's emergence as a star did not come until well into his third pro season. By that time, Earl Lloyd had succeeded Butch van Breda Kolff as coach and Lloyd had been succeeded by ex-Piston Ray Scott. The emphasis was turned from offense to defense, a notorious Detroit shortcoming for years, and the team began to look like a potential contender.

In 1973–74, Lanier's knee no longer nagging him as his weight stabilized in maturity at between 270 and 275 pounds, the Pistons became, for the first time, one of the NBA's powers. The club compiled the best record in its history, 52 wins against 30 losses, and reached the playoffs for the first time since 1961–62.

"Lanier's improvement since I've become coach is monumental," said Scott. "He has learned to pace himself, to play both ends of the floor. As for running out of gas, we've tried to take some of the burden away from him. There's a tendency with some stars to take charge in the first quarter, then not have anything left late in the game. But if you take the burden off a player and have good shot distribution and team defense, it helps him coming down the stretch.

"This whole thing relates to him. If your big guy wants to work for you every night, you're going to be a helluva coach. If he doesn't, you're a bum."

There were no more jokes about Lanier's monstrous feet. Rather, in his slimmed mode, chocolate-hued skin, and short, trimmed beard, intent on his work, he was a menacing figure who, perhaps more than any other basketball giant, seemed the personification of the Biblical Goliath. It seemed, I recall thinking as I saw him play one night, that with a suit of armor and a helmet, brandishing a battle-ax, he would indeed be a figure so awesome that none but an especially naïve shepherd boy might challenge him.

At midseason, Lanier scored 12 of his game-high 24 points in the fourth period to lead the West to a 132-123 victory over the East in the annual All-Star Game at Seattle, and he was elected the game's Most Valuable Player. At the close of the season, his personal statistics showed a scoring average of 22.5 points per game, down from his 1971-72 mark of 25.7, but he averaged 50.4 per cent field-goal accuracy and he ranked among the league's leaders in rebounds and shots blocked.

The Pistons' title aspirations were quenched by second-place Chicago in the first round of the playoffs, but Lanier's and his teammates' sharply improved defense and team play concluded things optimistically for the club for the first time in years. Lanier had improvements still to make in consistency and stamina and he was still outmaneuvered and outfoxed too often by clever older men such as Abdul-Jabbar and Nate Thurmond, but his potential was awesome.

/ / /

The problem in Detroit had been to wait for Lanier to mature in his range of skills and to control his girth before the team could become a contender. In Los Angeles, the problem was how to maintain championship level in the meantime, and the Buffalo Braves were seeking to emulate the Milwaukee Bucks' climb by accelerating their development from expansion club to respectability.

The answer for the long-established team and the young franchise came in a series of interrelated player maneuvers engineered by Eddie Donovan, the Buffalo general manager who had been the engineer of the New York Knicks' rise half a decade earlier (and who returned to the Knicks in 1975).

First, taking advantage of his success in the annual coin flip between last-place teams in 1971, Donovan drafted Elmore Smith of Kentucky State, a rangy youngster whose shot-blocking and rebounding had led a small, all-black college to the NAIA championship. He was inexperienced against tough competition, but the word in basketball is, "You can't teach a guy to be seven feet tall." Smith was the *best available big man,* and Donovan was hopeful of building his team around him.

The next season, Donovan and Coach Jack Ramsey pulled one of the neatest bits of enterprise in the league's history. Bob McAdoo, 6-foot-10 All-American at the University of North Carolina, had declared himself eligible for the pro drafts as a "hardship case," but was supposedly committed to the Virginia Squires of the American Basketball Association. The ABA commissioner, Jack Dolph, went so far as to write NBA teams, warning that McAdoo was not available to them.

"All Dolph's letter said," Donovan later recalled with an understandable hint of a smirk, "was that McAdoo had signed with the Squires. There was no proof that he had, and McAdoo was under twenty-one if he had. We did our homework on McAdoo. We got sound information from people close to the Squires that McAdoo had not signed with them. We didn't feel that we would take that much of a chance by drafting him."

Gasps were heard in other NBA executive suites when Donovan succeeded in signing the slender 21-year-old, and the gasps turned to painful grunts when he joined a front line which already included the promising Smith and burly, 6-foot-8 veteran Bob Kauffman. The Braves won only 21 games, but, offering a point of consolation, at least they were clearly superior to Cleveland and Portland, the two clubs which had entered the league along with them in 1970.

The mix wasn't quite right. Smith, uncertain in his grasp of Coach Ramsey's complex defensive theories, gave the team the chance to compete with respectability against teams blessed with star centers. Kauffman was a power forward capable of coping with the strong cornermen of the league. But McAdoo had difficulty chasing such small, high-scoring forwards as John Havlicek of Boston, Lou Hudson of Atlanta, and Jim McMillian of Los Angeles. McAdoo was the league's Rookie of the Year, but it wasn't considered that much of an honor that season, and, troubled by his tough match-up problems, he averaged only 18 points per game.

In Los Angeles, meanwhile, there was uncertainty over the status of Wilt Chamberlain. Two years in a row, Chamberlain had led the Lakers into the championship round, but now he was flirting with a six-figure ABA offer and the Lakers sought insurance against his departure. Donovan offered to give up Smith in exchange for the heady McMillian, and the Lakers, although aware of Smith's shortcomings, agreed to the deal. Limited as Elmore might be, he was a legitimate 7-footer and he offered brighter promise than anyone the Lakers might reasonably expect to draft within the next several years. There were the usual public claims that they were obtaining a super-star, but the organization was privately contented simply that Smith could play well enough to keep the team a contender if Wilt jumped to the ABA—as it seemed he had decided to do.

The Buffalo plan was to install Kauffman in the pivot and flank him with McAdoo and McMillian. As the season opened, though, Kauffman was temporarily sidelined because of a groin muscle pull and McAdoo filled in. The youngster's response to the opportunity to play in the more familiar pivot position was so immediate and so explosive he could not be dislodged. One high-scoring, high-rebounding, high shot-blocking night followed another, and, by the end of the season, he'd averaged 30.6 points per game to lead the league in scoring. He was the field-goal percentage leader, too, at 54.7, third in rebounding at 15.1 per game, and third in shot-blocking at 3.32.

Rookie Ernie DiGregorio was able to perform with much the same leadership and sharp passing he'd displayed as a Providence College All-American, and trades brought strength in power forward Garfield Heard early in the season, veteran bench strength in Jack Marin and Matty Guokas later. The sum of McAdoo's strong showing, the addition of DiGregorio, and the help provided by the trade-acquired personnel was a doubling of victories from 21 to 42 in just one season and the club's first appearance in the playoffs. Boston whipped the Braves in six games, but the word around the league was that Buffalo was clearly a team of the future.

"I was convinced last year I could play center in this league," McAdoo, only 22 years old, explained midway through his brilliant season. "It's where I've always played and I feel more at home there. On defense, it keeps me nearer the basket, where I think I can help the team more. On offense, I'm getting the ball more and I'm getting more shots from the middle."

He convinced the Celtics his scoring leadership was no fluke. "I never saw a shooter like him in my life," marveled Don Nelson. "What a great release."

Bill Nichols, San Francisco Examiner

Pivoting with agility despite his bulk on size-22 sneakers, Detroit's 6-foot-11 Bob Lanier dwarfs Golden State Warrior forward Cazzie Russell . . . and prevents him from moving toward the basket in early 1974. It was the season things fell together for Lanier and for his team

"There's no way I could guard him," added Paul Silas, the strong 6-foot-6 cornerman who was asked at times to switch off to McAdoo so that center Dave Cowens would not have to chase him. "He's six-ten and he jumps out of the sky. I bump him, and he still shoots over me."

Contributed Cowens, "He's a quick jumper. He doesn't seem to have to flex his knees before he jumps. He's up there before you know it."

In 1974–75, McAdoo retained his scoring title, helped Buffalo win even more games, and was named the NBA's Most Valuable Player. His days of hardship were clearly behind him.

/ / /

Los Angeles' situation was as agonizing as Buffalo's was exciting. Chamberlain's departure was pretty much decided by early September 1974. When the Smith trade was announced, Wilt felt rebuked and scorned by the team despite his contributions of the previous five years. Less than two weeks later, he was being introduced as the new coach of the San Diego Conquistadors.

Installing Smith at center and teaching him the Laker system was a major project, but it was only one of Coach Bill Sharman's many problems—professionally with the team and personally, tragically, with the horrible realization that his wife, Dorothy, was stricken with incurable cancer, which would take her life within a year.

Connie Hawkins came to the Lakers in a trade for holdout Keith Erickson to fill one forward berth, and second-year player Jim Price had to be worked into the lineup when All-Pro guard Jerry West sustained a severe abdominal muscle pull which kept him out of all but 31 games.

Nate Thurmond and the Golden State Warriors were expected to exploit Los Angeles' 1973–74 season. Instead, they fell back to the Lakers' level when 6-foot-9 forward Clyde Lee went out in November with a serious knee injury and did not rejoin the team until February.

Both the Lakers and the Warriors were stumbling as the closing days of the season neared. Smith led the league in blocked shots, but his scoring and rebounding were disappointments, he frequently got himself into foul trouble, and

Buffalo Braves

Bob McAdoo of Buffalo Braves, rookie of the year in 1972–73 and the league's scoring champion a year later

there were grumblings that the Lakers would have been out in front in the Pacific Division race if only he had played more assertively.

"I'm not Wilt Chamberlain," Smith retorted in an interview with Mike Morrow of the suburban Redondo Beach *Daily Breeze.* "Not even Wilt could do the things some people expect me to do. I'm being blamed because we're not in first place, aren't I? When I came to L.A., I thought I would learn some things that would help me in basketball. This is still a new game for me, but I haven't learned anything. I'm doing the same things now I did in college. I'm not at all satisfied."

There were recurring reports that the Lakers would offer a package of experienced players, cash, and future draft choices to Portland should the Trail Blazers win the coin flip for the rights to three-time All-American Bill Walton of UCLA. There could be only one interpretation—Smith was inadequate.

In the Bay Area, there was rejoicing when the Warriors

swept back-to-back games with the Lakers a week before the close of the season even though Thurmond had been idled by a badly sprained foot. All the Warriors had to do was win two of their next five games and the title would be clinched no matter what the Lakers might do.

Smith turned from tabby to tiger at this point. As the Warriors collapsed miserably with six losses in their next seven games, the Lakers kept winning (15 victories in their last 19 games, the final tally would show). Smith climaxed an astounding late-season surge by scoring 37 points against his ex-Buffalo teammates on March 24, 1974, in the game that clinched Los Angeles' fourteenth consecutive berth in the playoffs. He completed a streak of 67-for-107 field-goal accuracy in that win, and averaged 20 points per night over a five-game stretch that turned his muttering detractors into enthusiastic supporters.

"Elmore is unbelievable. He's incredible," burbled one of the Lakers' veterans, Happy Hairston. "I've never seen a player respond like he has. He has taken charge. He wants the ball. He's not practicing any differently and we're running the same plays. But he's something else. Why, he's coming down the court on the fast break and stuffing. I've never seen anyone stuff the ball quicker. He's also rebounding and blocking shots."

Said Smith, unaccustomed to the attention, "My role on this team was a defensive player and shot-blocker. When we weren't scoring against Golden State, I decided to do something."

His turnabout was mystifying, in other words, but heartily accepted. Kareem Abdul-Jabbar and the Milwaukee Bucks needed only five games to eliminate the Lakers when the playoffs opened, but just getting that far was considered accomplishment enough in so turbulent a season.

In the accounting and in the evaluation of what role Smith might play in the future, it had to be noted that his year with the Lakers was only his sixth in organized basketball. Only in his final year as a high-school student in Macon, Georgia, had he taken up the sport. After that had come just two seasons of eligibility at Kentucky State and his three years as a pro.

"I hate to keep saying that I had a late start that kept me

Elmore Smith uses his elbows, his weight, and his height to box out Milwaukee's Kareem Abdul-Jabbar on behalf of Buffalo Braves. Punishing contact like this every time a shot is attempted is the reason pros call the area under the basket "the butcher shop"

from being the type of player I want to be," Smith told Mal Florence of the Los Angeles *Times*, "but it's true. I make a lot of mistakes that I shouldn't make."

Said Sharman, "Considering his inexperience, he is probably a couple of years from reaching his peak. He has a tremendous amount of talent and potential. He is a great jumper with long arms and the ability to block shots—which is a very important category. If you can do this at the right time and know how to hold your position or get back to the boards, it's a great quality. This is what made Bill Russell great. Of course, Elmore isn't in a class with Russell as a rebounder, but I hope he'll keep improving. I think he is in the same class in jumping and blocking shots."

Jeff Mullins of Golden State was asked to explain the Warriors' inability to withstand the Lakers' resurgence. He confessed mystification. When he was asked about Los Angeles assets, he offered a ready reply. "Elmore Smith," the veteran guard asserted, "is the best shot-blocker in the league. He can jump off both feet, which isn't as easy as it sounds. Abdul-Jabbar, for instance, needs that one step. When you see him winding up, getting ready to jump, you know he's coming to block your shot. With Elmore, he can be standing flat-footed and still get up so high . . ."

/ / /

Smith's problems continued in 1974–1975, and there were accusations that his membership in the Jehovah's Witnesses religious group had somehow made him concentrate less completely on basketball than he should have. He alternated streaks of lackluster play with periods of brilliance, but, in a season marked by West's retirement and a succession of injuries, he was labeled a disappointment and the Lakers' run of playoff appearances ended.

New heroes emerged. Clifford Ray, only 6-foot-9, but tenacious and intense, alternated with shot-blocking specialist George Johnson, 6-foot-11, for the Golden State Warriors, and both of them were astounding as the lightly regarded team won not only the Pacific Division title but the Western Conference and over-all NBA crowns as well. Rick Barry was the Warriors' leader, but Ray's and Johnson's center play . . . their defense and their rebounding . . . were vital to an amazing team triumph.

Another 6-foot-9 player, Sam Lacey, helped Kansas City–Omaha make the playoffs for the first time. Bulky, willing Kevin Kunnert, a 7-footer from Iowa who had shuffled to new teams twice in his brief career, helped Houston make its first playoff appearance. John Gianelli continued to improve as New York reached the playoffs by defeating Buffalo on the final day of the season. Jim Chones, 6-foot-11, picked up out of the American Basketball Association, found a home in Cleveland and helped the Cavaliers to their best season.

These were not superstars, but they were giants, and they provided a solid base for teams just learning how to win. The league's remaining losers? They scouted the college and even the high-school ranks searching for a great big man of their own. The conclusion was unanimous throughout the sport: Winning starts in the middle.

HOORAY FOR THE RED, WHITE, AND BLUE: ARTIS GILMORE, BILLY PAULTZ, SWEN NATER, AND THE ABA

"It belongs in a circus—on the end of a seal's nose," sneered Alex Hannum, coach of the Philadelphia 76ers, the first time he was told that teams in a league called the American Basketball Association were going to play with a ball colored red, white, and blue. Not long afterward, Hannum was coaching a team on the art of shooting that funny ball through a hoop.

The league was born in a series of clandestine meetings among ambitious young promoters and petty politicians in Southern California in 1966. From the start, there were factions ambitious and eager to build independently and to reach parity with the National Basketball Association on pure merit . . . and opposition factions suggesting economies and contrivances to stay alive merely long enough to force a merger.

Franchises were born, transferred, buried, and reborn with the giddy frequency of a movie queen's succession of marriages and divorces. Players rotated from team to team nearly as rapidly as teams went from city to city. The ABA elevated all basketball salaries and bonuses into stratospheric realms in competition for talent, and the league reshaped for all time the comfortable rut the NBA had settled into during the mid-1960s.

In time, the shoestring-operating, tax-shelter-seeking owners of the early days gave way to men of substance. The new league began to grow in playing skill and in national recognition, even though the ledgers were written almost exclusively in the crimson ink of deficit spending.

The red, white, and blue ball helped. It provided a definitive trademark. Otherwise, all the teams could publicize was a group of relatively nondescript players who had failed in the NBA, retired from the NBA, or had never been invited to try out in the NBA.

Owners peddled the party line that its teams and players were just as good as the NBA's, but the propaganda was swallowed by neither the nation's news media, the fans, nor the ABA players themselves. They had no self-delusions.

ABA executives manipulated fiercely to woo established stars out of the NBA, but, for the most part, failed. Rick Barry did go from San Francisco of the older league to Oakland of the infant group, but his situation was less than typical; the general manager of his new club happened to be Bruce Hale—his college coach at the University of Miami and, more pertinently, his father-in-law.

Where the ABA faltered most in the early years, it seemed, was in the battle to sign outstanding players emerging from college. Particularly, they failed to land the type of player needed most to gain full respect: outstanding young centers.

The Kentucky franchise pledged to go all out to sign Wes Unseld off the campus of the University of Louisville . . . but he signed with Baltimore of the NBA instead. The Houston franchise boasted of how it would surely land sensational Elvin Hayes from the college in its home city . . . but he went to San Diego of the NBA instead. And the New York Nets were certain that Lew Alcindor would rather play for them in their arena out on Long Island, within easy commuting distance of his parents' apartment in Manhattan, rather than in the hostile land of the upper Midwest . . . but he signed with the Milwaukee Bucks instead.

In the ABA's first four years, in fact, only once had a leading collegiate center opted for the new league rather than the old. Mel Daniels, a native of Detroit who starred at the University of New Mexico, was drafted both by Cincinnati of the NBA and Minnesota of the ABA in the new league's inaugural season, 1967, and chose the ABA. Daniels, a rangy 6-foot-9 and 230 pounds, became the league's leading rebounder even as a rookie and helped the Muskies finish second to Pittsburgh in the playoffs. The next season, his salary too great for a floundering franchise destined to be transferred to Miami, he was sold to the Indiana Pacers in a deal engineered by Indiana's clever young general manager, Mike Storen. The deal paid immediate dividends as the Pacers climbed to the ABA championship.

By 1971, the ABA had shaken out its weaker cities and taken better hold in those that remained. The league had gained a bit of stature with the addition of two men—Zelmo Beatty, 6-foot-9, a seven-year NBA veteran who jumped to the Utah Stars, and rookie Dan Issel, also 6-foot-9, an All-American from the University of Kentucky who spurned the NBA for an ABA contract reportedly worth $1.4 million.

The emerging great big man out of the college ranks following Alcindor's graduation from UCLA was a bearded 7-foot-2 giant from Jacksonville University in Florida named Artis Gilmore. There was contention that 6-foot-11 Bob Lanier of St. Bonaventure was better, but the consensus among scouts was that Gilmore was the more mobile and the better player on defense, that he would probably make greater immediate contribution to his pro team than might the bulkier New Yorker. A youngster from Florida State, Dave Cowens, was attracting some attention—but he'd have to play forward in the pros, most people figured.

Gilmore, unlike Lanier or Cowens, had matured late, and was still maturing. He grew up in rural Dothan, Alabama. He was a 6-foot-8 center averaging nearly 40 points per game in high school, but attracted scant attention even from the bird dogs who survey talent on behalf of college teams. He was bypassed by the major schools and wound up at little Gardner-Webb College in North Carolina. There, grown to 7-foot-2, he was recruited by Joe Williams, a young coach trying to turn Jacksonville University of Florida into a national power.

While Williams was coaching transfer student Gilmore and

the rest of the Dolphins to high national ranking, an ownership change was occurring in Kentucky. A syndicate headed
by businessman Wendell Cherry bought out the original owners of the Colonels and, seeking new front-office direction,
sought the man who had made Indiana the most successful
team in the league—Storen. They offered the ex-Marine a
$50,000 base salary, bonuses for attendance and victories, and
also offered him the right to purchase stock. "If I owned the
team, I would never give out the contract that I have," Storen
laughingly admitted later.

More important than the inducements for Storen personally, they gave him virtually a blank check when it came to
going after talent. Money was a necessary weapon, it was
recongized, but, in Storen, the Colonels had something extra
going for them—savvy.

It was Storen who outbid and outnegotiated the NBA for
Issel and who thus helped the Colonels reach the ABA finals
in 1970 against Bill Sharman's Utah Stars. Issel was no match
for the NBA-wise Beatty of the Stars, and the Colonels lost in
a well-played championship series. There would have been
more attention paid nationally to the competition if the contending cities hadn't been so relatively obscure in contrast to
the NBA finalists of that year—Los Angeles and New York.

Even as the title series was being played, Storen was laying
the groundwork for his next, greatest coup. At midseason, the
ABA had held its annual preliminary "secret" draft. That is,
the proceedings were supposed to be secret; in observance of
ABA tradition, word spilled almost immediately to the news
media.

NBA teams chafed in anticipation of the draft. People
wondered whether Detroit or San Diego, flipping a coin for
the right to make first choice, would go after Lanier, Gilmore,
or NCA scoring-record-setter Pete Maravich of LSU as
number-one choice. And they wondered whether, having
drafted them, they'd be able to sign them.

Storen wasn't content to wait for the NBA proceedings. The
assumption was that Lanier, Gilmore, and other eligible seniors would wait for the NBA draft and bargain one offer
against the other before deciding which bid to accept. That
was, after all, the only logical business thing to do, wasn't it?

The NBA coin flip was still several days away and the collegiate playoffs had barely gotten underway when Storen made an announcement which remains a high point in the ABA's turbulent history. Gilmore had signed with the Colonels instead of waiting for the NBA draft, the stocky and aggressive executive disclosed. The salary, bonus, and deferred-payments deal amounted to "well over six figures," he added. Later, there was a closer pinpointing of the money involved—$2.7 million, a sum greater even than Milwaukee had agreed to pay Alcindor. "So much for the myth that the NBA always gets the big man," chortled Colonels co-owner Cherry.

One void in the Kentucky organization remained—the club needed a coach. One of Storen's first, most controversial steps had been to fire local hero Gene Rhodes after only 15 games. The replacement was one-time Boston Celtics "best sixth man in basketball" Frank Ramsey, but only for the rest of that season. Ramsey operated several business enterprises in Kentucky and was not interested in continuing with the Colonels even though he'd taken them as far as the seventh game of the playoffs. When the Lakers of the NBA fired well-liked Joe Mullaney early in the summer of 1971 and replaced him with Utah's Sharman, Storen hired the displaced man for himself.

Mullaney emphasized defense, and in Wilt Chamberlain in Los Angeles he'd had the gigantic, shot-blocking kind of man his pressuring, double-teaming, gambling style demanded. Gilmore, while a rookie and no rival to Chamberlain on the list of great pro centers, was at least of a similar *type*.

Wearing old-fashioned high-top sneakers, built with wide shoulders and especially muscular thighs, wearing a satanically cropped beard and cutting his hair in a billowing Afro, Gilmore was a strange-looking, even frightening, figure.

He was eager and aggressive, and he tried to block every shot that was taken within 10 feet of him, it seemed . . . even if he was called, again and again, for goal tending. There was little polish to his game, certainly little of the fluid grace and mental toughness of the man who was just then coming to be known as Kareem Abdul-Jabbar. Gilmore's presence permitted Issel to move to a roaming, power forward role. The two gave Kentucky an exceptional inside game that balanced well against the three-point goal-range outside shooting of flitting guard Louie Dampier. It was a slowed-down tempo game, but it was effective.

"Artis makes life a lot easier for me now," Issel told the New York *Post*'s Jim O'Brien in January 1972. "I don't have to worry about the rebounding so much, and he's made us all look a lot tougher on defense. I never saw Bill Russell in person, but I don't see how anyone can get as high as Gilmore."

Said Rick Barry, playing at the time for the New York Nets, "I played against Russell and Wilt and I played with Nate Thurmond, and I know how good they are. This kid can be the same sort of dominating player. He has a natural knack for defense. I should know. He blocked five of my shots in one game. Artis can shoot better, and when he learns how to play defense, where he has to go on the court, and so forth, then he'll be better than Russell."

Not even Gilmore would make so ambitious a claim, but the young man did not lack for self-confidence. "Every time I walk out on the court," he said, "I play to win. At a certain point, I have a feeling I *have* to get the ball. When you're continually getting rebounds, you feel it's automatic that you'll get the next one."

Said Mullaney, "There are times when his background surfaces," a reference to Gilmore's occasional sulks and pouts. "He hasn't been playing basketball very long, and he has played under a lot of different coaches. He's not prepared to handle some things that a more experienced man could handle. When he makes a mistake on defense, it seems to hurt his concentration on offense the next couple of times downcourt. When he gets things where he wants them, everything is fine. But he hasn't been exposed to enough pressure to be completely ready for it."

/ / /

While Lanier was playing spasmodically for Detroit and Maravich was performing wildly and unhappily for Atlanta in the NBA, Gilmore was becoming the ABA's most important player. The Colonels compiled a regular-season record of 68 wins against only 16 losses as Gilmore averaged 23.9 points per game, led the league with a 17.8-per-game rebounding average, and had close to 10 blocked shots nightly, too. For the first time, Indiana's Daniels was displaced as All-ABA center, and Gilmore further honored himself and the Colonels by earning selection not only as Rookie of the Year, but also as Most Valuable Player.

It was such a commanding individual performance that the Colonels finished an incredible 23 games ahead of Virginia in the division race. The team Storen had assembled was heavily favored to win the playoffs. Instead, beginning a pattern of frustration, the club was eliminated in the first round, four games to two, by the third-place New York Nets.

There was no sophomore jinx to bedevil Gilmore the next season, but he did not bring the Colonels to the top of the league, either. In the regular season, the Colonels finished second to Carolina. Gilmore, Issel, Dampier, and their teammates reversed things with Carolina in the preliminary playoff round, but lost the title to Western Division champion Indiana in a seven-game final series.

Kentucky's three victories over Indiana in the final round were almost completely Gilmore's work. He had, in order, performances of 29 points, 26 rebounds, and 9 blocked shots; 28 points, 16 rebounds, and 7 blocks; 29 points, 21 rebounds, and 2 blocks. In Indiana's four wins, Gilmore played well enough . . . but not superbly. Columnist O'Brien, covering the series for the St. Louis *Sporting News,* noted, "The guilty feeling must remain. Gilmore knows if he'd been overwhelming one more time, the Colonels would have been ABA champions for the first time."

Gilmore's third season as a pro was even more frustrating. It began with enormous enthusiasm and ambition. There had been two management shuffles in the off season. First came a sale to a group which intended to move the team to Cincinnati. Then there was a second sale which brought the club back to Louisville under the ownership of John Y. Brown, chairman of the board of Kentucky Colonel fried chicken, but under the active management of an all-woman board of directors headed by Brown's wife, Ellie. And it was not simply a token thing—Mrs. Brown and her cohorts took hold aggressively, increasing season-ticket sales and bringing direction to the front office.

Storen, however, was a casualty. He needed authority to handle problems himself and resigned rather than remain with limited power, a frustrated employee. Late in the summer, the Kentucky situation worked to the ABA's advantage when Storen was available to accept the commissionership when the position became vacant for the fourth time, before moving on once again to head ownership at Memphis.

Mullaney moved on to the Utah Stars, also apprehensive about the all-woman management group, and Babe McCarthy, a coach in the ABA since the league's first season, was hired to replace him. McCarthy noted Gilmore's defensive rebounding capability and the team's potential for quickness and decided that a running, fast-breaking game was in order rather than the methodical game Mullaney had played.

Brilliant forward Julius Erving, by 1973 the ABA's greatest publicity asset, led the young New York Nets to the Eastern Division championship with 55 wins compared to Kentucky's 53 in the regular season, but Gilmore had his best season personally and won the league rebounding title again with an average of 18.3 per game—his best mark yet. Late-season trades seemed to have improved the Colonels, and they were favored in the playoffs. They routed Carolina in the first round to reinforce that favoritism, but were shatteringly upset by the Nets in the division finals. McCarthy was discharged within a week after the final loss.

Gilmore prepared for a summer enjoying the unlikely hobby of scuba diving off Florida, along with his wife, Enola, and 18-month-old daughter, Shawna, but paused before leaving Louisville to express continued ambitions for the future.

"I want to be the greatest player who ever played the game," he said. "I don't know if I'll ever reach that objective, but I'm not being fair to myself or my team if I don't point in that direction. I feel a man should have only one goal. And that is to be the very best. I don't believe in personal goals, isolated goals which relate to a game or a season. If you do that, and you accomplish these goals, then I feel you lose your incentive. If you reach the top of a mountain, there's no place else to go so you set your sights on the highest mountain and hope someday you'll reach it."

The league was consolidated at ten teams for 1974–1975,

and a rebuilt Denver franchise, the Nuggets (the old nickname, "Rockets," was dropped to signify a new beginning) dominated regular season play. Kentucky was a power in the East once again, but the Denver club was considered the coming franchise.

Hubie Brown, formerly assistant to Larry Costello at Milwaukee in the NBA, became the latest in the succession of Kentucky coaches. Several good trades were engineered. The Colonels won with a power game and opportunism, and replaced New York as No. 1 team in the East.

In the playoffs, Indiana, rebuilt with a corps of fine young players and led by devastating forward George McGinness, upset Denver to earn the right to meet Kentucky in the championship series.

It was an opportunity for Gilmore to try to climb his mountain once again . . . and this time he reached the summit. He was magnificent in three straight playoff victories over his long-time tormentors, scoring 41 points and adding 28 rebounds in a 109-101 third-game victory at the new Market Square Arena in Indianapolis, including 13 points in the final period. "Artis," marveled McGinniss afterward, "that's the best game he's ever had against us."

McGinniss and his teammates gathered themselves to keep the series alive with a victory in the fourth game, but the series returned to Freedom Hall in Louisville on May 23 and Gilmore surpassed himself. The Colonels captured the championship with a 110-105 victory when Gilmore scored 28 points and added 31 rebounds, an ABA playoffs record.

"These guys were really hungry because not one of them had ever played on a championship team either in college or pro ball," Coach Brown said with elation. "They were so hungry they won 22 of their last 25 games, including four out of five against Memphis, St. Louis, and now Indiana in the playoffs."

Said Issel, "Maybe we can shed this 'loser' tag once and for all."

Added Indiana's assistant coach, Jerry Oliver, looking at the statistics and hearing word that Gilmore had been the series' most valuable player, "We tried everything to contain him, but we couldn't and that was the series."

McGinniss added, "People have said Artis is not a good pressure player. Well, he proved different in this series. He just dominated it."

/ / /

If Gilmore has been the ABA's leading center by so huge a margin, it has not been because rival teams have failed to seek men to challenge him.

Carolina thought it had a man to match him in Jim Mc-Daniels of Western Kentucky, but learned expensively he wasn't the guy.

Roy Boe, owner of the New York Nets, paid a small fortune to woo a 6-foot-11 youngster named Jim Chones off the Marquette University campus, but sold him off to Carolina a year later and was further disillusioned when Carolina cut the players loose on waivers in the spring of 1974 and saw him be picked up by the NBA's Cleveland Cavaliers. There, with maturity, Chones began to realize his potential . . . but too late to reward Boe.

Dr. Leonard Bloom of the San Diego Conquistadors made the boldest move of all—he bargained Wilt Chamberlain away from the Los Angeles Lakers and made him player-coach only to be blocked by enforcement of Chamberlain's NBA contract. He wound up paying Wilt close to $1 million to serve just as his coach and, by the spring of 1975, had been forced to give up the franchise.

The status report on the ABA in the summer of 1974 showed Gilmore pre-eminent, with New York's hulking Billy Paultz, San Antonio's Rookie of the Year Swen Nater, Indiana veteran Mel Daniels, and slender San Diego rookie Caldwell Jones the best of the rest.

Paultz grew up in New Jersey. He had a fair prep record, but wound up at Cameron Junior College in Oklahoma rather than at a major college. Teams in the metropolitan New York area apparently weren't interested in a baby fat–heavy center who wasn't a great shot-blocker. But he could score, and he returned from Oklahoma to the East Coast to play well at St. John's of Brooklyn before failing in a brief NBA tryout, then hooking on with the Nets.

By taking advantage of his outside shot and his bulk on

Billy (The Whopper) Paultz scores for the New York Nets

defense, "The Whopper" neutralized Gilmore in the 1973–74 playoffs and played a key role in the eventual championship-series victory over Utah.

Nater's arrival in basketball was also belated. He was born in Holland and didn't begin to play basketball until his high-school days in Long Beach, California. Good grades and his near 7-foot size made him a good prospect for UCLA out of Cerritos Junior College, and he reached a dim sort of national fame by being the reserve who mopped up after Bill Walton and the first team turned most games into routs.

Nater's shooting and aggressiveness were evident even in brief appearances, however. His senior season, he was selected along with teammate Walton to play on a United States All-Star team for a national tour against the Soviet Union. He distinguished himself against the Russians and was drafted on the first round of the NBA draft by the Milwaukee Bucks.

The draft had seriocomic overtones. He had played infrequently at UCLA because Walton was on the squad. Going to Milwaukee, it was felt, he would be benched again in favor of ex-Bruin Kareem Abdul-Jabbar. Actually, Milwaukee had greater plans for him than that.

General Manager Wayne Embry, an ex-center himself, saw Nater as a power forward who would team with Abdul-Jabbar to create a front line with both size and extreme fire power. Before Embry could reach Nater and explain what he had in mind, the ex-Bruin signed to play with Virginia of the ABA. Less than two months into the season, he was sold to San Antonio and went on to become one of the best young players in either league.

San Diego's 6-foot-11, 210-pound Jones was a surprise. One of three giant-sized brothers, Jones played at little Albany State in Georgia and was drafted by Philadelphia of the NBA on the second round. The 76ers felt they had a true sleeper in the slender youngster from the Deep South, but, when he asked a huge bonus-salary deal to sign, chose to let him go elsewhere.

The elsewhere was San Diego, whose coach, Chamberlain, had good information from his original home town (Philadelphia) that the kid was a good one. Jones got his chance when

Chamberlain was restricted only to coaching in court action brought by the Lakers.

He rewarded Wilt by playing vigorously and precociously. Jones averaged better than 13 rebounds a game, better than 15 points per game, and averaged four blocks per game, finishing second only to Nater in balloting for Rookie of the Year.

Would Gilmore, Paultz, Nater, Jones, and their ABA contemporaries earn national recognition in time as equals to the men who played in the NBA? Would the ABA survive as a separate league? Or would it merge with the NBA or even collapse altogether? There were only questions in the summer of 1975, not answers. As great as is the demand for centers, however, one thing was certain: as long as they chose to make playing basketball a profession, there'd be places for the ABA's better big men somewhere.

10

MAGNIFICENT FAILURES

Gene Wiley's fingers were slender . . . tapered . . . delicate . . . long-proportioned even for a man who stands 6 feet, 10 inches tall.

"Gabby," as he was called by his teammates because, of course, he was shy and introspective, spoke hardly more often than to call out to one of his Los Angeles Lakers teammates as they played defense together, "Pick left . . . watch it right . . . I've got the dribbler!"

His complexion was the delicate creamy brown of the finest Swiss milk chocolate. The features were well chiseled and, in his playing days of the mid-1960s, the hair was cropped neither too short nor too long.

Slender, but wiry-strong at 210 pounds, Gene was especially effective defensively for a team led by Elgin Baylor and Jerry West and which preferred, if it could, to win games 140-130 rather than piddle around with too much defense and win by 102-89. Gene's job was to let it *be* 140-130 instead of 140-145, and he performed it with a quiet, mechanical competence.

There was a tragic aura about Gene Wiley, and no moment in his brief career in basketball characterized this man better than a meaningless, but oh so poignantly revealing, moment in Boston one late winter afternoon in 1966.

A sportswriter named Harris was covering that road trip for the Los Angeles *Herald-Examiner,* and invited a couple of players to join him for a quick lunch at the team's hotel after a flight from Philadelphia.

Wiley accepted the invitation with a murmur of thanks and a nod of his head. Jim King, a steady backcourt player from Tulsa University who now coaches at his alma mater, was ready for a sandwich, too.

The three of us, Jimmy and I chattering about a mildly successful road trip for a team which had already assured itself a berth in the postseason playoffs, stood in line together at the coffee-shop entrance, waiting to be seated on a busy afternoon. Patrons at nearby tables inside the velvet restraining rope stared at the three of us . . . the super-tall Negro, the not-quite-so-tall, slender fellow, and the shorter, more talkative fellow wearing eyeglasses.

We paid no attention to the quizzical looks. Used to the endless travel of the NBA, we'd gone through the same sort of thing too often with too many different combinations of players, coaches, radio broadcasters, and newspapermen to take much notice.

We were shown to a table, finally, and picked up our menus. It took Wiley just a moment to decide all he wanted was a hamburger, a small salad, and a cup of tea. Something other than hunger commanded his attention.

As a centerpiece on a table surrounded by the same plasticized kind of nondescript decor found in thousands of coffee shops, there stood a simple, clear-glass vase which held one long-stemmed red rose.

Gene Wiley, a man who earned $18,000 a year in physical combat with such men as Wilt Chamberlain, Nate Thurmond, Wayne Embry of Cincinnati and, that night, the mighty Bill Russell, stared for a moment at that flower, shutting out in his wonder at its beauty all the extraneous chatter and tawdry banality of his surroundings.

He studied the flower. Truly, deeply studied it. Then he reached out, with the same delicate fingers that were so adept at swatting down basketballs, to bring the rose toward him. He studied it a bit longer, perhaps noting the symmetry of the petals and enjoying the sweetness of the perfume. Finally he brought the rose even closer and inhaled deeply in slow, sensual appreciation.

King and I stopped our chattering. We remained silent rather than intrude on the haven that our friend had created for himself out of a single lovely rose. He'd left, for a moment, the painfully cruel world of athletics in favor of a world he enjoyed much more deeply.

Born and raised in the black ghetto of Amarillo, Texas, and recruited by a number of colleges for his height and for his basketball potential rather than for his fineness as a man or for the gentility of his soul, Gene Wiley earned his living playing basketball.

At Wichita State University in Kansas, which he'd selected because major schools in his home state were not ready yet to enroll black athletes, he was told to take easy courses so he'd

Los Angeles Lakers

Gene Wiley worked hard at basketball, but really wanted to be an artist be sure to stay eligible for basketball. Like many athletes with similarly limited educational backgrounds, he wasn't able to take the same advantage of college opportunities enjoyed by schoolmates from more favored home and community environments.

Mostly, he played basketball. He'd have preferred to work on his sketching or on his color sense or on other skills demanded of a serious artist.

His Laker career was brief. He played only from the seasons of 1963–64 through 1966–67 . . . four years. His heart wasn't truly in his work, and, more tragically, his knees locked in an arthritic debility shocking in a man so young. Dr. Robert Kerlan, the famed Los Angeles orthopedic surgeon, said as the Lakers announced Wiley's premature retirement that vitamin deficiencies in his boyhood, coupled with his zooming physical growth as a boy and then the overexertions of big-time college and pro basketball, had left him with a chronic disability. Wiley might continue to play basketball, but at risk of being half-crippled the rest of his life.

/ / /

Today, two huge oil paintings hang in the corridors of the Los Angeles Lakers' offices in the bowels of the Forum. The craftsmanship is slightly crude, demonstration of the artist's unperfected technique. But the eye is sure, and in the determined faces of Elgin Baylor and Jerry West, the franchise's two great stars, there is all the fire and intensity of their models.

The paintings were commissioned by Laker owner Jack Kent Cooke, first because he wanted heroic-sized oils of Baylor and West as dramatic embellishments for the Laker offices, second because he chose to assist in the least-demeaning possible way Wiley's painful transition from star athlete to struggling, largely self-taught painter.

No one with the Laker organization is sure now just what became of Wiley. "He's back in Amarillo . . . I think," said one of General Manager Pete Newell's assistants.

Wiley stands in memory, thus, as one of a legion of ambitious, tall young men who have come to professional basketball eager for success because the game was the best career opportunity open to them.

Some fail because their bodies are not quite large enough, after all, or not quite strong enough. Others fail because, with ample bulk, there is insufficient quickness and spring in their legs. Many fail, as did Wiley, because they lack the mental toughness to compete against the single-mindedness of their rivals for places on the team . . . or because, having reached the pro level, their bodies could not keep up the pace.

The mystique of the 7-footer repels and attracts. High-school and college coaches seek sometimes to intimidate opponents. They take a player who is 6-foot-8 or 6-foot-9 and proclaim him as a 7-foot-0. If the player has sensitivity about his height or about his clumsiness or about economic deprivation, a coach may seek to soothe the ego at the expense of building the man.

/ / /

Another player who passed briefly through the Laker organization—he passed briefly through a number of organizations—was Billy (The Hill) McGill. He came from Jefferson High in Los Angeles, a school located in a grimy, dirty, semi-industrialized black ghetto in east-central Los Angeles. The dropout rate was appalling and reports of incidents of violence there made students at other Los Angeles schools in the early and mid-1950s shudder for fear the problems would spread. Two decades later, they did. Riotously.

Two things provided pride and an example for accomplishment at Jefferson High. For one, a man named Ralph Bunche had been a student and athlete there once and had even become student-body president in the days when Jefferson was a primarily white, primarily middle-income neighborhood school. The other example which students might follow was a tradition of outstanding track-and-field athletes and outstanding basketball teams . . . sports requiring relatively low investments in equipment or uniforms.

Billy McGill, sleepy-eyed and gawky, entered Jefferson as a 6-foot-8 tenth grader. The rumor spread quickly through Los Angeles' basketball underground that Jefferson had "this great seven-footer" who for sure was "going to make Jeff city champs." A sportswriter quickly dubbed him "Billy the Hill," an echo of the earlier "Wilt the Stilt" of the East.

Under the coaching of since-retired Larry Hansen, a gentle

white man from North Dakota who stayed at Jefferson as late as 1972 because of his understanding of values in athletics greater than the merely sporting at a school such as this, McGill blossomed. He and his teammates won City championships three of his four varsity seasons and lost in the title game the other year.

Billy had a supremely accurate, unique shot he'd fire from the baseline to the right of the hoop. His back to the basket, he'd lift himself on his left foot and half hook, half jump a short-trajectory arc which almost always found its target.

Hansen coached more than just offense—he platooned sets of five players at a time, operated a full-court-press defense, kept his players and the opponents scrambling. With derision, opponents called Jefferson's game "jungle ball" . . . but they felt it a moral victory, usually, to lose to the "jungle bunnies" by fewer than 20 points. McGill could do more than merely shoot, and he helped Jefferson students be proud despite all their personal and family difficulties.

Naturally, despite minimal grades, McGill was widely recruited. He stood a fraction over 6-foot-9 when he left Jefferson, although he was still referred to as a 7-footer. His only contacts with the white world outside the mid-city ghetto had come on the basketball court, not in classroom competition or in social situations. He was withdrawn and shy.

He chose the University of Utah as his college destination, not fully advised of Salt Lake City's strong Latter-day Saints Church influences or recognizing that adjustment to an all-white society, to college, and to big-time basketball simultaneously might be an enormous challenge.

He didn't fail. The reports are that his fine-arts-major classes were structured for him so that he'd stay eligible. While he had few black companions to seek out socially, his basketball success as a great scorer made him at least a celebrity whose needs and problems were usually met by schoolmates or Utah boosters.

The offense and defense were designed to utilize his height and to set him up for his unblockable hook jump from the baseline. He was *assigned* to take the majority of his team's shots. Not surprisingly, in his senior season—1962—he averaged 38.8 points per game (second best in history at the time) to lead all collegiate scorers.

He was selected an All-American on a team which also honored such future pro fixtures as Jerry Lucas of Ohio State, Chet Walker of Bradley, Lennie Chappel of Wake Forest, and Terry Dischinger of Purdue. A fellow named John Havlicek, an Ohio State teammate of Lucas, was deemed good enough only for the second team.

Just one pro league existed at the time—the NBA. Its Chicago franchise, created through expansion for the 1961–62 season, chose McGill on the first round of the draft and Dischinger second. Four other rookies were in preseason camp, too, and all six were to bid for places on the final roster. Basketball had failed in Chicago earlier and the franchise was on trial. So was Jack McMahon, the coach, a ruddy-faced ex-playmaking guard who'd been a starter on the St. Louis Hawks's great teams of the late 1950s.

Convinced by his sycophantic rooters and boosters at Utah that he was a special person, having left the poverty of Jefferson High behind him, McGill came alone to the bargaining table with the Chicago Zephyrs' management. Agents hadn't entered sports yet. He asked not for a normal contract that stipulated so many dollars per season and an additional bonus for signing, but, instead, demanded to be paid by the point! It was preposterous, and he agreed—after coaxing—to a conventional sort of deal.

McMahon needed instant performance from a ragtag sort of team whose major asset was 6-foot-11—a *true* 6-foot-11—Walt Bellamy, the previous season's Rookie of the Year. It was Bellamy for whom things were structured now, not McGill. Rather than being a pampered star, he became a mop-up player who entered games when the outcome already was decided. He played just 590 minutes (compared to Bellamy's 2446) and averaged just 7.2 points per game.

Thrust into a cruel pro world in which players were expected to take care of themselves and not to need special attention, he seemed bewildered and lost. If he ached, it was up to him to ask the trainer for treatment, not for the coach and trainer to seek him out. If housing was difficult to locate,

San Francisco Warriors

Billy (The Hill) McGill failed in pro basketball following a brilliant collegiate career at the University of Utah

that was his problem, not the team's. Billy's problems were not created by poor intelligence, but by the difficulties he found coping with the NBA and with a society too busy to give him special attention.

The week the 1963–64 season opened, McGill was traded to New York for a fading veteran guard named Gene Shue and a hulking 6-foot-9 ex-Cincinnati University All-American who'd flopped as number-one pick of the Knicks, Paul Hogue. It wasn't a bad season. Billy averaged 15.1 points per game as a reserve center . . . but he became expendable when the Knicks drafted centers numbers one and two in the draft, the number two being a fellow named Willis Reed. The Knicks traded him to St. Louis for a second-round draft choice and cash, all but giving him away, and his psyche was so bruised by then he was cut early in the season.

Billy clung to basketball. It was the only life he knew. He managed to get into the Midwest's semipro Continental League, and it was from Grand Rapids that he was picked up— exhumed—by the Lakers in January of 1965.

The Lakers continued to have center problems at the time,

Wiley's knee becoming more and more a concern, and McGill was still a local legend. He was worth a try.

McGill didn't travel for road games, a pre-Jack Kent Cooke ownership-era economy. Instead, he spent hours in a neighborhood gym trying to regain his self-confidence and his shooting touch, lost someplace during his travels. He hadn't been much of a rebounder or defender or passer since high school because he'd not been asked to do much at Utah except shoot, and now even his hook jump was failing him, a further attack on his ego.

McGill finally was added to the traveling roster for the playoffs, and made only a token appearance as the Lakers lost the world championship to Boston. Players clustered in hotel lobbies and in coffee shops, but Billy, lost and sensitive, was usually alone.

The last trip to Boston during the playoffs was his last appearance in a Laker uniform. A year later, he failed in a tryout with the San Francisco Warriors and, three years after that, he failed to earn a job in a tryout with the Los Angeles (later Utah) Stars of the then-young American Basketball Association. And today, he's back in Los Angeles struggling for a dollar like other men of approaching middle age—black, brown, and white alike.

The two memories I'll keep of Billy McGill are of his high-school days, when he could rebound some and defend some and shoot that hook jump of his so softly and so straight. And I'll also remember a night in the summer of 1965, when he was trying so hard to hold on with the Lakers.

Most of the players lived in Southern California year-round in those days, and Coach Fred Schaus (now coach at Purdue University) held weekly off-season workouts.

A local college coach named Paul Thomas had befriended Schaus and mentioned, in passing, that he was working toward a Ph.D. in advanced aspects of physical education involving muscle function, physiology, and similar deep, deep topics. What interested Schaus was Thomas's report that he'd devised a series of exercises effective in developing muscle tone and strength, yet requiring no special equipment or expense.

The exercise program was isometric in nature, building

strength by making muscles work against resistance, yet not
making muscles too bulky or too inflexible. The program
called for two players to help each other, one the activist and
the other bracing to provide the resistance. And then the two
could switch roles.

Schaus invited Thomas to demonstrate his system at one of
the weekly sessions. Jerry West, Elgin Baylor, Rudy LaRusso,
Wiley, and others gathered around as Thomas and a volun-
teer, a young Laker from UCLA named Walt Hazzard, demonstrated how to build arm strength, leg strength, jump
higher, develop greater stamina.

The players watched in fascination, and there were mur-
murs of agreement that the program had much to offer,
particularly during road trips when players could go through
them without having to take barbells, pulleys, or other special
equipment along with them.

McGill, knowing full well his place on the roster was in
jeopardy, yet as interested as the rest of the men, watched
intently.

"So you see, guys," said Thomas, "these are some ways you
can get stronger and fight fatigue by helping each other as
little as ten or fifteen minutes a day. Any questions?"

West asked for an exercise which might help keep his
hamstring muscles supple. He was always pulling the darn
things. Thomas, assisted by Hazzard, complied.

Baylor asked for an exercise which might speed his recovery
from knee surgery. Thomas obliged.

Finally, there were no further questions. And Thomas
asked one more time, "Anything else?"

At the rear of the group, a slender brown arm went up.
Softly, almost apologetically, Billy McGill asked solemnly,
shyly, "Do you have any exercises for just one person . . .
alone?"

Thomas replied politely—in the negative—and those of us
there who liked Billy, who hoped for him to find himself and
his career, shuddered silently at the poignancy of the request.
How terribly alone, how terribly lost poor Billy must have
been. It was a moment of anguish to recall as balance against
other times and other places when other men, more fortunate
and more talented, celebrated their success.

Portland Trail Blazers

LaRue Martin had the height, but not the bulk or strength, to fulfill the goals Portland set for him after selecting him above all other collegians in the 1972 draft

/ / /

Money was the root of McGill's problems . . . not enough of it in his family when he was a boy, not enough of it because he could not make it when he became a man. Too much money can be equally destructive, especially in the current era of exaggerated bonuses and salaries.

In 1972–73, the expansion-formed Portland Trail Blazers won the postseason coin flip which determined which of the NBA conference's tail end teams would choose first in the draft. Portland won, and then rejoiced that it would have the opportunity, as other expansion teams before it, to become a contender by taking the country's best incoming big man.

Given a nation from which to choose, General Manager Stu Inman and his scouting staff decided that their man was 6-foot-11 LaRue Martin of Chicago's Loyola University . . . a player who had averaged 19.5 points per game and 15.7 rebounds per game as a senior, but whose national reputation was minimal. What seemed to have attracted Inman's eye was a pair of fine midseason performances, back to back, against Marquette All-American Jim Chones and UCLA's all-time all-star Bill Walton.

Around the big hotel ballroom in which the draft was being held, there were suppressed giggles and looks of surprise. Martin weighed only 200 pounds. He had not been expected to be named early because of his deficiencies in weight and strength.

Having drafted Martin, however, the Trail Blazers were in a uniquely contemporary quandary. They could only hope he'd grow to become the center who would make the club respectable, yet to fail to sign him would mean embarrassment to the franchise at home and a propaganda loss to the entire league should its number-one draft choice sign, instead, with the rival ABA. Martin's value, therefore, exceeded by a vast amount even the most optimistic predictions by the Trail Blazers of what he might ultimately mean for the team in only win-loss considerations.

Of necessity, the team based much of its ballyhoo during the off season on the arrival of a 6-foot-11 center, downplaying as much as it could the fact he was so slightly built. Veteran players resented the $1 million-plus contract he was able to wangle, and fans—by now sophisticated about interleague warfare—were sceptical at the claims the team made on his behalf.

In less insane times, Martin might have been drafted further down the list, been offered the opportunity to add bulk with maturity and, perhaps, helped his team in due time. Now, he was force-fed, literally and figuratively, with basketball lore and with food.

Martin reported to training camp . . . and simply was not ready. On the bench, he was three-dimensional proof every night that the Trail Blazers had drafted unwisely and paid him even more unwisely. An unheralded 6-foot-7 rookie from Tennessee State, Lloyd Neal, was pressed into service as center while Martin languished on the bench except for brief, hooted moments. Later in his career, he had several fine games, but they were rare.

The definitive evaluation of LaRue Martin, number-one

draft choice among number-one draft choices of the entire NBA, was delivered by jolly little Dick D'Oliva, trainer for the Golden State Warriors, in the coffee shop of the Washington Plaza Hotel in Seattle the afternoon of a preseason exhibition doubleheader in 1972. The Trail Blazers trooped in for their pregame meal and D'Oliva, at a nearby table, looked long and studiously at Martin, head to toe, as the bedeviled rookie passed by.

"You know," marveled D'Oliva, an NBA veteran who shared the generally held view that drafting Martin first had been a painful blunder, "that kid could tread water in a test tube!"

/ / /

Too much money too early and with too much fanfare also is regarded as a reason for the failure of Jim McDaniels, at this writing considered the most expensive mistake in pro sports history.

For three years at Western Kentucky University, McDaniels was acclaimed a sure-fire future pro star, a 7-footer with a feathery shooting touch. Pro scouts drooled at the prospect of so agile a giant, although they debated heatedly whether his natural position as a pro should be center or forward . . . and whether he would choose to play in the NBA or in the ABA.

The second issue—which league he'd choose—was a false one. As early as November of his senior year, McDaniels secretly signed a contract committing him to the ABA, although, at that point, the team for which he would play had not been determined. Western Kentucky won the Ohio Valley Conference championship and went on to finish third in the NCAA playoffs while NBA teams considered him and the ABA clubs laughed behind closed doors.

When the ABA finally revealed a secret midseason draft, it was disclosed that McDaniels had been drafted by the Utah Stars. Then, even before the NBA staged its own selections, the Carolina Cougars, in an announcement puzzling even in the dizzy world of pro basketball, announced they'd signed him!

Two separate turmoils ensued.

First, there was revulsion and anger within college ranks that McDaniels apparently had played for Western Kentucky

after he actually had become a pro. Western Kentucky ultimately forfeited its third-place NCAA finish and returned
more than $66,000 to the NCAA as its share of championship
playoff proceeds.

The second controversy boiled within the ABA as the Stars
sought to enforce their claim on the youngster and as Carolina
fought to keep him. A settlement was reached, finally, and
McDaniels hastened to Greensboro, North Carolina, for what
was expected to be a noteworthy professional career.

"Ten years ago," McDaniels told interviewer Mitch Mitchell
early in his rookie season, "I was shining shoes for a quarter a
lick. Now, I've been to seven different countries [on trips
sponsored by the State Department], have a college education,
built two playgrounds for kids [in his home town of Scottsville,
Kentucky], got my Cadillac outside, live in a ten-room house,
and I'm a millionaire. Sometimes I say to myself, 'Lord have
mercy! How did I do all this in such a short time?'"

With part of the bonus money he was given for his initial
signing with the ABA and for agreeing to play for the Cougars, McDaniels bought a home for his mother in Scottsville as
well as a home for himself and his wife in Greensboro. He
banked and invested much of his salary, a frugality prompted
by his youth as one of seven youngsters raised in a rural
community by a widowed mother.

His boyhood was marked by deprivation and hunger, but
he was not scarred to the point of inarticulate rage or overt
hatreds. Rather, he was well spoken and generally well liked
by teammates and fans alike as a rookie pro struggling—with
apparent success—to learn how to play a winning brand of
center.

The early notoriety ebbed and he became one of several
high-priced people playing in the less-publicized, less-fol-
lowed ABA. He wasn't tearing the league apart, but he was
among its best scorers, at 26.8 points per game, and he had
given General Manager Carl Scheer and owner Tedd Munchak reason to feel their investment in him was sound.

In February 1972, after McDaniels had barely missed being
named Most Valuable Player in the ABA All-Star Game, the
Cougars arrived at Dallas's Love Field for a game with the
since transplanted Chapparals. The Seattle Sonics of the NBA

Jim McDaniels warms up with his fellow Seattle Sonics before a 1973 game ... and before return to the bench as a nonstarter. He was cut by Coach Bill Russell even though he was—and is—one of highest-paid athletes of all time

were at the airport, too, on a brief stopover en route East, and McDaniels accidentally encountered Spencer Haywood. The Sonics' star had begun his career in the ABA, but jumped later to Seattle following lengthy and historic litigation handled by Los Angeles attorney and sports agent Al Ross.

The two players exchanged gossip and complaints, as players will. Haywood suggested Ross's services when McDaniels complained about financial problems: he didn't feel his original agent, Norman Blass of New York, had provided him with sufficient tax shelters, and he was concerned that his contract did not offer enough safeguards that he'd ultimately get all the money the Cougars had promised.

Contact was made between McDaniels and Ross, and on February 10, 1972, the mod-dressed, glib-talking lawyer was in the Cougars' office in Greensboro to present a list of 18 complaints, including a request for a special $50,000 bonus for the "aggravation," as a black man, of having to play in North Carolina.

Tom Meschery, now assistant coach of the Portland Trail Blazers, a sensitive former NBA star who was a published poet and whose zeal for the sheer joy of playing basketball long had marked him as an anachronistic throwback to the game's pioneering era, recalled the next development in a book, *Caught in the Pivot.* It was about his year as Cougars coach and about his subsequent disillusionment with the sport.

"I called Mac into the office," Meschery recalled. "I asked him point-blank what was going on. I pleaded with him to level with me. I asked Mac who his beef was with—his ex-agent, Blass, or the Cougar management. He said that it was a contract problem. So this business about taxes was only a subterfuge. Something bigger than taxes was going on. I felt sick at my stomach. Mac was trying to get out of his contract. That had to be it.

"I asked Mac if he was planning to leave town. He answered that if he didn't get 'things' straightened out that afternoon he was going to Los Angeles. I asked how he could leave his teammates? Couldn't it wait until the end of the season, only twenty-five games away?

"Showing no outward emotion, he said that it was a matter of principle.

"I did not want to go into it any further. There was no feeling between us any more. Maybe there had never been on his part. I had a deep affection for Mac. I saw, with some hard work, the makings of another Bill Russell. Perhaps it was the similarity of their voices, or the way he walked, or the proud way he carried himself. There was something there that was great. Here was the hell of losing somebody with whom you thought a real communication would develop.

"I cut off our talk. There were eleven other players to worry about who were now warming up out on the floor. I would know all the details soon enough. I left Mac, asking him to promise to call me if things weren't resolved that afternoon. He promised to call. He never did. That was the last time I was to see or talk to Jim McDaniels."

In swift succession, there were announcements in the next few days that Ross considered McDaniels's contract with the

Cougars void, that a new contract had been signed with Seattle (which had claimed NBA rights to him in what had seemed an empty gesture), that McDaniels would join the Sonics immediately . . . and that the Cougars had filed suit to block the shocking jump from one league to another.

Ross's arrangement with ambitious owner Sam Schulman of the Sonics, paralleling at slightly lower figures the contract worked out between them when Haywood jumped from Denver of the ABA to Seattle, called for $1.5 million over the next six seasons, none of it in deferred payments and none of it contingent on mutual-fund growth, investments, or other iffy considerations agreed to between others players and other teams. In turn, Ross was to help McDaniels with investments which would provide the tax shelters and security.

There was little public sympathy for McDaniels, Ross, or the Sonics. In fact, there was national outrage at McDaniels's ruthlessness and selfishness. It had been alleged, among other complaints, that he was unhappy with Carolina because the steering wheel on the Cadillac the team had purchased for him did not have an adjustable tilt!

An out-of-court settlement was reached later between Schulman and the Cougars, and McDaniels was left with the new problem of how to cope with rival centers in the NBA. Twelve games were left on the schedule, and McDaniels— jeered by fans and treated as an exotic curiosity by NBA reporters—managed to average only 9.4 points per game, less than 8 rebounds per game.

He began the following season as starting center under a new coach, Tom Nissalke, but soon demonstrated too little a regard or capability for defense or rebounding to stay in the lineup, too little finesse in shooting a center's close-range shots even to perform well at least as a scorer. His long-range jump shot and agility decreed he should have been a forward . . . but Spencer Haywood was his team's shooting forward already, and Schulman had too huge an investment in him to permit his coach to bring McDaniels along as slowly as his limited abilities ordinarily would have dictated. The final tally for the dismal 1972–73 season, halfway through which Nissalke was fired, showed McDaniels having scored just 5.6 points per game as a little-used, highly paid reserve.

The final humiliation came less than a year later. Schulman coaxed Bill Russell out of the broadcasting booth and into the dual role of general manager and coach of the Sonics. Familiar with the team's personnel because he'd broadcast several Sonics games, Russell announced early in his tenure that McDaniels would henceforth be a forward, Haywood the center. To prepare for the transition, McDaniels agreed to spend June and July of 1973 playing in a semipro summer league against other young pros in Los Angeles, and he was optimistic when Russell's first season began. Again, he was assigned tentatively as a starter . . . but soon, as Russell found winning infinitely more difficult as a coach than it had ever been for him as a player, McDaniels was back on the bench.

In January, shockingly, Russell announced that McDaniels had been cut from the team, but that the terms of the much-debated contract would still have to be honored. Bitterly, McDaniels returned to Kentucky to hope something might be worked out that would permit him, still a young man, to play basketball. And Russell emerged as that much greater force for integrity, so strongly dedicated a coach that he was able to convince a title-hungry owner to pay more than $150,000 per year for an ill-starred adventure rather than attempt to compound a mistake with further false hope.

/ / /

It was the quest for the great big man and the ambition that his arrival would mean championships and profits which elevated Jim McDaniels's costs so far above his true athletic value. If Tedd Munchak of the Carolina Cougars and Sam Schulman of the Seattle Sonics had not so fervently yearned for a dominating center for their teams, McDaniels might have been brought along slowly, less expensively, and, in time, become an outstanding player.

Walt Bellamy's career lasted nearly four times as long as McDaniels's and he ranks among the all-time NBA leaders in scoring and rebounding. Yet, in the sense of success as championships and self-fulfillment, he has been a failure, too.

He played, in turn, for the Chicago Zephyrs and Baltimore Bullets (the franchise was transferred in 1963), for the New York Knicks, for the Detroit Pistons, and for the Atlanta Hawks. Each move was marked by acrimony and divisiveness

Walt Bellamy bobs and weaves for an opening for Atlanta Hawks . . . and can't find it because of Dave Cowens' blanketing defense behind him, exaggerated hope and unfulfilled ambition ahead of him.

He was a brilliant collegian at the University of Indiana at 6-foot-11 and 245 pounds, the best college center in the country in 1961. His arrival in the pros ought to have been a heralded, welcomed circumstance. Instead, it provoked bitter turmoil within the NBA.

Acquired by New York from Baltimore in 1965 as a step—so it was assumed—toward making New York a power, he instead touched off new controversy and forced Willis Reed out of the center position and into three years of unhappiness as a relatively clumsy forward.

Acquired by Detroit from New York in 1968 as a step toward making the Pistons a strong team bulwarked by its first truly great center, he instead became a constant reminder to his management and his team's fans of how hornswoggled Detroit had been in the deal. To get him (and reserve Howie Komives) the Pistons had given up Dave DeBusschere . . . and DeBusschere became the man, replacing Reed at forward and permitting Reed to return to center when the position was vacated by Bellamy, who made the Knicks finally, blissfully, the world champions.

Acquired by Atlanta in 1970 to provide leadership for a team possessing good mobility and scoring punch, Bellamy instead continued a career-long pattern of inconsistency and recurrent lethargy which puzzled not only his team but also himself.

There seemed no reason that a man with his size and leaping ability, possessed of strength for the inside game and a feathery jump shot for outside scoring, should not have been an all-time all-star. Thoughout his career, in contrast to what had been expected of him, he scored 35 points one night, 8 the next . . . pulled down 20 rebounds one night, 5 the next.

After one of his "on" performances for the Knicks in February 1968, Willis Reed marveled, "If he does it every day, we could be the best. I wish I knew why he doesn't."

Coach Richie Guerin, whose Hawks had been victimized by Bellamy and the Knicks that night, joined in the discussion of the mystery. "That big moose . . . he can do anything . . . if he would," said Guerin. "He's as coordinated, as strong, as agile, as fast as anybody. He really can run. But if you can get it in his head, you're a magician."

Said Bellamy, as mystified as those around him by his in-and-out performances, "I try. Believe me, I try. But sometimes it can't happen."

Such is the mystique of the great big man that, two years after his partly complimentary, partly damning comments about Bellamy, Guerin negotiated successfully with Detroit to get the ex-Hoosier for the Hawks. When Pete Maravich came out of LSU to join Bellamy and All-Pro forward Lou Hudson in the fall of 1970, Guerin and the Hawks expected elevation to the heights of NBA power. Instead, internal strife and inconsistency continued. By 1973–74, Guerin had been fired as general manager and Bellamy continued a center of controversy for the new management team of Pat Williams in the front office, Cotton Fitzsimmons as the coach.

Early in the 1973–74 season, Fitzsimmons praised Bellamy and explained how he "handled him" as a simple matter of paying him the respect a pro of his tenure deserved. By the close of a disappointing season, however, the Hawks were so disillusioned by Bellamy that they actually forced the infant New Orleans team to make him their expansion draft selection off their roster. The agreement—without precedent in sports—was the sweetener of a deal which sent Pete Maravich to New Orleans as the new team's first player. In midsummer, humiliated by the Atlanta-New Orleans agreement, Bellamy retired.

His ultimate place in pro basketball history, at that, will have nothing to do with anything he has done—or not done—since his emergence from college. Without scoring a point or pulling down a rebound, he was responsible for a historic decision which had far-reaching influence on every team in the league, every team—including New Orleans—destined to join the league, and every player destined to become eligible for future drafts.

In 1961, as he went about rewriting the Indiana and Big Ten record books, two things had become apparent in the NBA. First, it was recognized that he was the best big man eligible for the draft that season. Second, it was agreed that the time had come to expand the NBA from only eight to, at least, nine teams. A group of Chicago businessmen sought a franchise for the nation's second largest city, and the NBA was prepared to grant the wish. For a price, of course.

An expansion draft system was designed to stock the new team with fringe players drawn from the eight existing teams. This was easily agreed to and created no particular dilemmas. But what about the collegiate draft? Should the new team draft first of all, as pro football had permitted its expansion teams to do in order to make them competitively respectable as soon as possible? Or should it wait until the established teams had taked their first-round turns?

The New York Knicks and their president, Ned Irish, argued fervently for the latter procedure. The Knicks were the worst team in the league at the time, had failed to improve themselves with opening first-round draft choices the past few years, and eyed Bellamy hungrily as potentially the great big man who might help them end their last-place embarrassment in a city craving competitive respectability.

Other owners and general managers argued that it was in the existing teams' self-interest to permit Chicago the first choice, since, with Bellamy, Chicago would be a satisfactory gate attraction. NBA teams' incomes come solely from home-game ticket sales, not from sharing road receipts, and a weak expansion team could not be expected to sell as many tickets as it traveled through the league as a Bellamy-led team might.

Chicago's interests—and the financial interests of the league—were upheld. The Big Bell went to the Zephyrs and immediately became a star player. The Knicks, without a top-flight center, continued to flounder. And to be bitter about it.

The NBA did not expand again for five seasons. Then it began a wave of virtually annual expansions from 10 to 12 to 14 to 17 and, by the fall of 1974, to 18 teams.

Has wisdom prevailed? Have expansion teams been given opportunity to become competitive quickly by permission to pluck from among the best of incoming college talent? Of course not. The Knicks' anger at being deprived of Bellamy's services was duly noted, and the pattern was established for subsequent expansions that all incoming NBA teams be consigned to agony their first seasons before beginning to climb.

Thus, even with turmoil around him unrelated to his personal guilt, Bellamy's historical significance must be regarded as a negative. Despite all his points and all his rebounds, he continued to disappoint himself, his teammates, and his employers. He has been, for the purposes of this chronicle, a failure . . . magnificently so.

11

THE WAVE OF THE FUTURE:
BILL WALTON, THE COLLEGIANS,
AND THE KIDS

The basketball season runs, for most Americans, from Thanksgiving day to just before Easter. In the colder climates, the season may be intense and widely followed. In warmer cities, the season may be just an interlude between the frenzy of football and the leisurely pace of baseball.

There is a special breed, however, for whom the basketball season lasts 12 months each year, four weeks each month, 24 hours each day. They are Gym Rats . . . the basketball underground . . . the people who know, seemingly by an alchemy denied less dedicated mortals, all the players and all the teams that play basketball in the land.

They are people like Nathan (Feets) Broudy, a shambling, comfortably sloppy man from Brooklyn who operates the 24-second clock for the pros at Madison Square Garden. He hasn't missed a Knicks game in years, and when he has free time he spends it watching high-school and college games or taking note as a dozen kids play a pickup game in the park.

They are people like Sam Davis, a sometime longshoreman and nighttime recreation league referee who haunts the little gyms and the big arenas of Southern California. He is always there when basketball is played, and he reached absolute nirvana for a Gym Rat the year he was official scorekeeper for a long-dead American Basketball Association team called the Anaheim Amigos.

Another of the breed is Avrum Dansky, a slowly-graying bachelor who works on the sports desk of the Los Angeles *Times*. For more than 20 years he has kept detailed records on high-school basketball players, including their height and weight, where they go to college, and whether they graduate eventually to the pros. The files crowd his apartment, take hours of his time—yet he toils for no profit or reason other than the personal gratification of being within that inner circle of truly completely well-informed basketball nuts.

/ / /

The great, continuing, abounding pursuit for these dedicated few is the discovery of talent in obscure places long before the names begin to appear in the national news media.

It is one-upmanship so subtle and so refined for the true *aficionado* that it has become almost ritual.

"Thirty-eight for Walton," Dansky might have mentioned, ever so casually, to Davis one day, long ago, had they met up in the bleachers at a junior-college tournament in Glendale or in some other Southern California town.

The challenge, the finesse of the game, would be, first, to know who "Walton" might be, his personal and season statistics, how well regarded he might be as a potential collegian and pro, and then—most important of all—whether "Walton" was Caucasian or black. The Gym Rat places no value judgement on race—yet this is important data in the litany of basketball. It is a measure of style, probably, and background.

"Yeah," Davis might respond to Dansky, "he got thirty-eight—but he was only twelve for twenty-five from the floor. Way off. Got the rest of his points from the line, and he only had twelve boards [rebounds]."

Point for Dansky—he could cite a recent game point-total for a little-known high-school junior who played 100 miles away.

Point, counterpoint, trump, and triumph for Davis. He'd known the name, known the game ... and had a more detailed set of statistics to cite!

Gym Rats never refer to players by full names. That would make the game too simple. The great, glorious times come with the emergence, now and then, of the particularly gifted young athlete with a particularly exotic name: *Wilt* . . . *the Big O* (for Oscar Robertson) . . . *the Big E* (for Elvin Hayes) . . . *Billy the Hill* . . . *Elgin* . . .

Happiness turns to joy and builds to ecstasy for the Gym Rat when the newest player to know is a potential great big man. The Gym Rat knows the value of a giant, and he watches as they come along—at first all elbows and kneecaps, awkward and self-conscious, and gradually smoother as the high-school career goes on. The youngster gets mentioned, in time, by the local newspaper's high-school reporter, and the Gym Rat pounces upon the citation with great glee; it is *de rigueur* to read all the out-of-town newspapers he can afford. One Gym Rat tells another.

The editor of a pulp basketball magazine, one of a dozen published each October, picks up the name and lists the boy among "America's Top 1000 Preps" in tiny type. A newspaperman in another city, reading through the magazine, notes the listing and writes a note or two. Soon, the underground picks up the emanations and the details and, somehow, the latest future "super" is soon known from Seattle to Miami and from Bangor to San Diego, wherever Gym Rats congregate.

In time, if the player's accomplishments begin to match the rumors and the claims, the general-circulation sports magazines take note and, by the time he's a senior, he becomes the topic of a film clip on the network television news those weekend 11 o'clock nights that run short of murders or politics. Finally, *Time* and *Newsweek* and *Sports Illustrated* take note, and an 18-year-old boy becomes a national celebrity.

/ / /

Bill Walton started that way at Helix High in the white, middle-class suburb of La Mesa, a bedroom community a few miles east of downtown San Diego. Reports on his prowess were greeted sceptically at first as overly parochial because the shot-blocking, high-scoring, gangly junior was (a) from an area not noted for basketball rather than from a crowded inner-city ghetto, (b) red-haired and white-skinned rather than Afro-maned and black, and (c) so prosaically named.

Bill Nichols, San Francisco Examiner

Three-time All-American Bill Walton of UCLA . . . clean-shaven, trim-haired and knee-bandaged . . . passes to an open teammate at Oakland Coliseum in March of 1973. It was a game against California . . . and another easy Bruin triumph

One of four youngsters in a sports-minded family fathered by a district chief in the San Diego Public Welfare Department, Ted Walton, the boy grew six inches between his freshman and sophomore years and three more the year after that. The spurt was so explosive it left his knees susceptible to hurt, and an operation was necessary to repair torn cartilage when he was 15.

The operation left young Walton gimpy and awkward. Intensely competitive, he learned to compensate for his temporary loss of speed by working hard at rope skipping and other exercises which developed his coordination and agility. He also became precociously adept at recovering opponents' missed shots and making the long passes which ignited his team's fast break. At 15, he was mastering the play some men never learn in 10 years as pros!

Helix won 49 straight games after a loss midway through Walton's junior season, dominating San Diego-area competition in a way no other team had ever managed to do.

The knees continued to be problems, however. Tendinitis developed, and Walton learned he had to use heat before every game, ice packs afterward. Still, his promise was so great that the Walton family was besieged by would-be recruiters representing scores of colleges. Telephone calls had to be screened and the number changed every few months or the family would have had no peace at all. It was a distasteful, tedious time . . . but it was endured in recognition that America treats all its outstanding young athletes this way, not just a family named Walton.

On the East Coast, Tom McMillen, also tall, also white, also a good student, the son of a small-town Pennsylvania doctor, was being put through the same ordeal. Mansfield, Pennsylvania, being closer to New York than La Mesa, the burden was even greater for McMillen. He had been discovered by the Gym Rats earlier than Walton, and he became the focus of the full national attention paid his year's "best college prospect in the country."

With a minimum of fanfare, Walton decided he would go to UCLA. An older brother, Bruce, was a 6-foot-5, 265-pound tackle on the Bruin football team. UCLA offered a fine academic program. UCLA was the dominant team in college basketball. Coach John Wooden had demonstrated his skill at utilizing and developing a big man's skills guiding Lew Alcindor to three NCAA championships in a row. And UCLA's proximity to Southern California's playlands and beaches was special lure for a boy with a love for warm weather and simple, outdoor recreation.

McMillen's decision came less tranquilly. He announced first that he would attend the University of North Carolina, then, mysteriously, changed his mind the day he was to have enrolled. The final, revised choice was Maryland—his father's first choice and the school at which an older brother, Jay, had been a 6-foot-7 All-Atlantic Coast Conference forward.

To the Gym Rats, it was a foregone conclusion that, in their first varsity seasons, McMillen and Walton would oppose each other in a Maryland–UCLA final for the NCAA championship.

The confrontation did not materialize.

Maryland had hired ambitious Lefty Drissell as its coach, and he openly admitted his goal was to make the school "the UCLA of the East." He recruited outstanding young players in addition to McMillen, but his team turned out only "good" instead of overpowering. McMillen, apparently having recorded such astounding high-school records in part because he'd begun to mature physically at an earlier age than most giants, never did develop the strength to play center full time and had to be shifted to forward.

Three thousand miles away, Walton blossomed. In his first dozen varsity games, he obliterated any thought of a rivalry with McMillen. Instead, he was soon being compared to Alcindor, Bill Russell, and the game's other all-time greats. He blocked shots, he gobbled up rebounds, he scored points, he played fierce defense . . . in short, he dominated.

Like Alcindor before him, he came to the varsity along with a group of outstanding teammates—including slender, smooth 6-foot-7 forward Keith Wilkes—and UCLA continued unchallenged as the best college team in America.

At 6-foot-11, 225 pounds, and 19 years of age, living alone for the first time and pressured constantly by newsmen seeking to interview him, Walton was the emerging superstar athlete attempting to cope with fame.

As early as this beginning stage of his career, however, Walton began to establish himself as a unique individual with depths and energies uncommon to sports heroes. Sensitive to society's problems and the injustices he felt were prevalent in America, majoring in history and taking Black Studies courses at a major metropolitan university noted for its liberal bent, Walton took on attitudes and outlooks transcending the boundaries of the Pauley Pavilion basketball court. He shied from interviews, but, when he granted them, was painfully outspoken.

"I'm not on a crusade," he said in March 1972, two weeks before completing a perfect season and leading UCLA to a sixth consecutive national championship. "I don't think the world can be saved. I think the biggest problem is racism. People can't accept the fact that some people are black, some yellow, some brown, white, and red. The whites have gotten it into their heads that, because they're white, they're right. They think that everybody else is wrong. You can't exist that way. You have to look at everybody as individuals.

"I think color has a lot to do with interest in me," he continued in a conversation with Bud Furillo of the Los Angeles *Herald-Examiner*. "It's been so long since there's been a white player who makes people say, 'This player's good.' You have to realize that people who support basketball are white, upper-middle class. So the white fans dig on me because I'm white."

Furillo probed further.

"Material things don't mean too much to me," Walton said. "I live in a small, one-room place—alone. I don't like to be with people I don't know because they're too obsessed with the fact that I'm Bill Walton of UCLA instead of my just being a person. I have a bunch of friends I spend most of my time with. I don't go to parties just to party. I like to go where I know everybody and they don't hassle me about everything. Then we're just people."

In his political activism on campus and his participation in antiwar rallies, he was unique among the sports heroes of recent years. Yet, like Kareem Abdul-Jabbar and Wilt Chamberlain and baseball's Willie Mays and football's Joe Namath, he struggled to maintain his privacy.

"I realize I can't keep my whole life private," he complained. "My basketball life is open to everyone, but what I do off-court for my own recreation and entertainment is my own business. I do what I want to do. People don't have to know. Even Coach Wooden doesn't know what I do.

"Everybody expects me to be a certain way. They have their idea of what a college ballplayer should be like—short hair and all that—but I'm not like that. I'm myself. I love long hair. I wish Coach Wooden would let us wear it as long as we like to have it. Some people would really be surprised. They think the UCLA team is a bunch of All-American boy types. But we're really not. I'm trying to have fun in life and not worry about what other people think."

The easiest part of his life was the basketball. His sophomore season concluded with a 30-0 record including an NCAA championship-finals victory over Florida State. His junior season, Walton still developing physically and in better control of a sometimes short-fused temper, the Bruins went 30-0 again. The final victory, again for an NCAA championship, marked Walton's finest collegiate performance—in fact the finest collegiate game ever played by anybody.

With an entire nation looking on, Walton singlehandedly demolished a good Memphis State team, 87-66, at St. Louis. He was a huge cat around the basket, tipping in teammate's misses and converting lob passes into spectacular, leaping layups. He shot accurately from mid-range distances, too. He finished with 21 field goals in 22 attempts and with a pair of free throws for 44 points, more than any other player had ever scored in an NCAA final. He also had 13 rebounds and played his usual dominating game defensively.

Walton wasn't available to newsmen, despite their pleas, after the incredible performance. While defeated Coach Gene Bartow and others were calling Walton "the greatest college player of all time," the 6-foot-11 redhead was pushing his way through reporters and a gathering of would-be well wishers on his way to the exit. "I've got to see some friends, man," he muttered before dipping through the St. Louis Arena doorway.

Later, it was learned that Walton's rush was back to the Chase-Park Plaza Hotel for a distasteful, but necessary, meet-

ing with Irv Kosloff and Don DeJardin, respectively the owner
and the general manager of the Philadelphia 76ers. Their
team had won the NBA coin flip and would have first pick in
the 1973 draft.

No college junior in earlier years had had to cope with
professional offers along with the routine, predictable pressures of classwork and publicity. But the ABA-NBA war had
warped the values and changed the patterns of the system.
Undergraduates were now fair game.

The ABA simply reached out and plucked the players it
sought who accepted the inflated contracts they were offered.
The NBA adopted the easily manipulated protocol of a "hardship" draft in which nonseniors could claim financial difficulty, then become eligible for selection and signing.

Walton's was no "hardship" situation, but he was far from
wealthy and the 76ers could have made an acceptable case. A
youngster offered hundreds of thousands of dollars would
have to be excused for agreeing to sign a professional team
contract rather than staying in school.

Kosloff described the Chase Hotel meeting later in an
interview with David Wolf of *True* magazine.

"We've given Mr. Gilbert a signed offer," Kosloff recalled
having said to Walton, referring to the Pacific Palisades contractor Sam Gilbert, who had befriended so many UCLA
athletes and who had assisted Kareem Abdul-Jabbar in his
negotiations four years before. "We think it's extremely sub-
stantial," Kosloff continued. "But, Bill, we hear you haven't
even looked at it."

"That's right, sir," said Walton.

"Don't you even want to know how much we're offering
you?" Kosloff asked.

"Sir, I'm flattered that you offered me a contract," Walton
was quoted as having replied. "And I'm not really rejecting it.
I'm just reaffirming the position I've had all along—that I
want to remain a student at UCLA until I graduate."

The 76er executives, their first and best hope for rebuilding
from the catastrophe of a 9-win, 73-loss season dashed, went
home to Philadelphia.

"The only thing I remember about that meeting," Walton

later recalled, "was wanting to get the hell out of there and go have a beer with my friends."

The day after his domination of Memphis State and of his brief meeting with Kosloff and DeJardin, Walton confirmed for newsmen that he had not given serious consideration to leaving school.

"I am not playing pro basketball next year," he said. "I have decided there is plenty of time left to earn a living, but now is my time to be a young man. All the attention and the publicity and financial bonanzas are not for me or my life. I don't need any reasons for coming back. I'm here and that's it. Money has not been a factor—I wish people would understand that. I dig change for the better, but I'm not changing now. My six months as a basketball player are over. Now I get six months to be a human. I want to get away and get some reality into my life."

/ / /

When classes finished in June, Walton's wanderlust led him to bicycle through the Sierras. He narrowly missed death late in the summer when he was stung by a bee and suffered a rare allergic reaction which required urgent medical attention. The incident left no permanent damage, but he was warned to carry a syringe of antitoxin with him on future trips into the wilderness.

By his senior season, his physique had filled out to a solid 235 pounds and the line of his chin and shoulders was defined. He was a man, no longer a gigantic boy. He reported to UCLA picture day bearded and with long hair. He drew a warning and suspension from Wooden, who ordered that his locks had to be shorn and his face clean-shaven before he would be permitted to join the team. The mini-rebellion against Wooden's strict rules lasted just one day.

The victory over Memphis State had marked UCLA's seventy-fifth consecutive intercollegiate victory. The once seemingly unchallengeable mark of 60 straight wins set by the Bill Russell-led University of San Francisco teams of 1955–56 had fallen the month before, and there were predictions as Walton's senior season began that the Bruins might record 30 more wins in a row. Every preseason listing had UCLA number one in the nation, as usual, and tickets for a UCLA home game were as hard to come by as publicity photographs of Raquel Welch de-emphasizing her bosom.

The UCLA students who lined up hours before the arena doors opened and the Bruin alumni who prized their season tickets saw little difference in Walton or in the team as the 1973–74 season began with its predictable collection of one-sided wins. The Bruins still played a harrassing full-court-zone press. Offensively, they still set up in their one-three-one offense designed to exploit Walton's multiple skills at low post. Some faces had changed from season to season, but it was the same John Wooden precision and the same frenetic madness in the stands. UCLA fans were never content with victory, they wanted humiliation for their opponents, and often were frustrated because Wooden and the players were satisfied simply to play well.

"Some people have weird priorities," Walton said early in his final UCLA season. "They'll build places like Pauley Pavilion while other people are starving. Adults will go berserk at our games. I used to be contemptuous of them. Now I understand the role reversal. They're trying to identify with us. But, really, man, they just don't have anything to do with us. Our priorities are the team's, not theirs."

Privacy meant more and more to him, and although he remained intensely concerned about society and the nation, he was more cautious about expressing those concerns in public forums.

He had discovered new serenity in transcendental meditation—observing 20-minute quiet periods twice each day—and by becoming a vegetarian. "I don't need drugs. TM gives you a better high naturally," he said. "It's beautiful. It makes you calmer. You see things differently. You realize that what matters is how you feel, right now, not how much money somebody wants to give you to play ball in six months. You see what a joke a lot of things like that are."

There was additional serenity for Walton because, for the first time since he began to climb in height, his knees were not cause for worry. The opening of Red China to the West had introduced acupuncture therapy to the United States, and

Walton underwent regular treatment which minimized the inflammation and pain that had plagued him for so long.

/ / /

If circumstances were relatively tranquil for Walton, they were bustling for the wheeler-dealers of pro basketball.

In San Diego, Dr. Leonard Bloom owned ABA rights to Walton and was hopeful he might eventually sign the La Mesa youth. Getting home-town superhero Walton might save the Conquistadors for San Diego . . . and/or enhance the franchise's value in a possible sale.

The NBA considered, at one level, Walton's superb playing skill, considered his publicity and propaganda impact at another.

Walton had proclaimed his unwillingness to play in a cold-weather city, and this had renewed Dr. Bloom's optimism. The NBA had a choice to make: (a) bend established draft procedure to enhance the probability of keeping him out of the ABA; or (b) follow traditional procedure and hope for the best. The same choice had been made as Lew Alcindor approached graduation, after all, and he had signed with Milwaukee even though that decision had seemed unlikely at the time.

Rumors flourished. Jack Kent Cooke was willing to trade three or four established players for the rights to Walton, it was said, The ABA would pool resources to sign him, as it had done to assist Dr. Bloom in signing Wilt Chamberlain. A new franchise would be formed to play in the Los Angeles Sports Arena; Walton would be offered part ownership, and his Bruin pals would come along with him to form the nucleus of the team. Walton's knees were so bad, he'd never play pro ball anyway. The networks were just waiting on Walton, went another rumble. If he signed with the ABA, a lucrative contract was waiting that would put the younger league on a national network for the first time.

Walton must have heard the rumors and rumbles, but he refused to respond. "Money doesn't buy happiness," he said. "I don't need it. Not even for food. I can live in the woods and eat berries. I've done it—hitchhiking and camping in the summer—and I've been happy."

In mid-December, UCLA faced its first crisis of the campaign. North Carolina State had gone 27-0 the previous season, but was ineligible for the NCAA championship because it was on probation for recruiting violations. Wolfpack rooters claimed superiority to UCLA, but had had no chance to prove it.

Arrangements were made for a meeting of the two powers at a neutral site—St. Louis Arena—with ABC's "Wide World of Sports" eager to televise the game nationally at rich profit to the two schools and their conferences. North Carolina State had a giant-sized center in senior Tom Burleson, a 7-foot-4 veteran of the United States Olympic team, and a brilliant 6-foot-4 junior forward in David Thompson. The game was expected to be classic.

Burleson played well. He forced Walton to the bench with his fourth personal foul late in the first half. But UCLA's overall depth and poise were too much. Walton finally returned to combat with $9\frac{1}{2}$ minutes remaining and the score 54-54. He turned on the power, dominating the rebounding and stymieing the N.C. State offense. UCLA opened a 73-56 gap and went on to a breezing 84-66 triumph.

The vanquished team fell to number three in the wire-service polls while a big, strong, aggressive Notre Dame team became number two. Anticipation mounted as the late January semester break drew near, when UCLA and Notre Dame would play home-and-home games. A nonconference rematch within a single week was unprecedented in college basketball, but Athletic Directors Moose Krause of the Fighting Irish and J. D. Morgan of UCLA, along with Coaches Digger Phelps and Wooden, had agreed to the arrangement because of the potential income. Both games would be nationally televised, and both schools had big new on-campus arenas they could jam with fans.

Two weeks before the pair of games, the Bruins suffered a major fright. In a game against Washington State at Pullman, Walton moved toward the basket to receive a lob pass from guard Greg Lee and bank it into the basket. It was a play at which Walton and Lee were especially adept, and which opponents usually found undefensable. This time, though, Washington State forward Rich Steele took position under the basket and Walton, leaping high into the air, tangled his legs with the Cougar, then fell awkwardly and with a sickening thud backward over him and to the floor. Walton writhed in pain. Finally, shakily, he was helped to his feet and actually returned, later, to the game. He missed the following weekend's pair of Pac-8 Conference victories, but announced by the time of the Notre Dame series he was ready to play.

The Saturday afternoon of January 19, 1974, was as emotional and tradition-abounding at South Bend, Indiana, as any football Saturday in the school's glamorous athletic history had ever been.

UCLA came to Notre Dame having won 88 consecutive games and seven consecutive national championships. Three years earlier, the Bruins had come to South Bend with 47 consecutive wins, hoping for 60, and had been defeated. One year earlier, the Bruins had come to South Bend with a new run of 60 consecutive wins and needed only one more—which they then got—to surpass USF and become the winningest college team of all time.

The epic outcomes of UCLA-Notre Dame games of the past helped build the national anticipation.

Walton hadn't played basketball for 12 days. He wore a corset to protect his back. The Bruins, unlike Wooden's pre-Pauley Pavilion-era teams, had played primarily at home early in the season. They were uncharacteristically nervous playing before a hostile road crowd. Still, UCLA played with its normal precision. The Bruins shot 70 per cent from the floor during the first half, Walton leading the way, and they led with 3½ minutes to play in the game, 70-59.

Then playing away from home began to tell. Notre Dame scored. The Bruins tried to stall out the clock, but threw away the ball. They seemed confused on defense. With 29 seconds left, Notre Dame had made 10 straight points and trailed by just one point. Little-regarded Dwight Clay worked into the open in the corner, took a pass, and lofted a soft, accurate jump shot which held up for a 71-70 Notre Dame upset victory.

"We'll get a better measure about the two teams after next

Saturday's game," Wooden said calmly after the pandemonium of the Notre Dame fans' final buzzer celebration had subsided.

"They played a good game. They won. That's all we can say," said Keith Wilkes.

Two days after the game, the weekly Associated Press and United Press International polls were published. Notre Dame was ranked first. North Carolina State was second. UCLA was only third.

It was a circumstance to challenge an entire campus, an entire community. Supremacy in college basketball was more important to sophisticated Westwood than students and alumni cared to admit. The week's wait for the chance at vindication against the Fighting Irish seemed endless, and a 6-foot-11 senior who liked to think of himself as blasé about sports found himself wound up in excitement.

"Walton's been psyching himself all week for this game," said Larry Farmer, a three-year varsity starter who remained at UCLA as assistant coach of the junior varsity. "He gets like this only a few times a year, but when he does he's unstoppable. He wants it, and don't let anybody fool you. The whole team wants it, too."

Banners at Pauley Pavilion on game night demonstrated UCLA's impertinence toward anyone brash enough to usurp the Bruins' role as best team in the land. "Hail Mary, Full of Grace," proclaimed one sign, "Notre Dame Is Second Place!"

Walton led the Bruins onto the floor for their pregame warmups. After the layup drills as a unit, the players began their individual shooting. Walton was taking 20-foot hooks and driving to the basket.

"Everyone could sense his intensity," said freshman Marques Johnson. "It spread so rapidly, we couldn't believe it. Suddenly, Keith was doing the same thing. Then Dave Meyers picked it up. You would have thought this was the finals of the NCAA."

Not surprisingly, the game was a rout, 94-75. Walton played so ferociously he fouled out with five minutes still to be played. But that was trivial. By that time, the Bruins were 26 points in front and Walton had scored 32 points (he shot 16-

for-19 from the floor), added 11 rebounds, and had been a marvel playing beneath the UCLA defensive basket, blocking shots and intimidating any Notre Dame dribbler foolish enough to contemplate a drive.

"They tell me that he practices harder than most ballplayers perform," said Notre Dame's Phelps good-naturedly. "I guess we got him angry by beating UCLA back there. Whatever the pros pay him won't be enough. He dominated every phase of play. How many times do you see that kind of performance? He scored thirty-two points without ever getting to the free-throw line. I think we've discovered his weakness. He doesn't draw fouls well."

At Notre Dame the week before, a banner had read, "God Wants Notre Dame To Be No. 1." At Westwood, a banner responded, "The Lord Giveth, but the Bruins Taketh Away."

/ / /

Something happened, unaccountably, to the Bruins after their devastating performance against Notre Dame. North Carolina State kept winning, pressuring UCLA for national ranking, and when UCLA was upset on consecutive nights at Oregon and Oregon State in February, the Wolfpack climbed into the number one ranking for good. Walton played well, but the Bruins seemed stagnated. Their full-court zone press no longer terrified opponents. They did not have their usual poise on the road. Teams found they could force UCLA's offense out toward mid-court and play to keep the ball from coming to Walton. Opponents refused, in short, to shatter and play dead before games even began as they often had done in the recent past.

UCLA had to go to the final game of the Pac-8 Conference season before clinching the championship with a victory over arch-rival USC. And, in the opening round of the NCAA regionals, the Bruins needed three overtimes to get past Dayton before drubbing USF for the Far West title and the right to go to the finals once again.

The championships were played at Greensboro, North Carolina, an easy riding distance from the North Carolina State campus, and the Wolfpack and their fans were primed to prove that their leadership in the wire-service polls was no mistake. It would be UCLA vs. N.C. State in a national semi-finals, and, while the Bruins would be favored, there was no inevitability about it. They'd played too poorly since the Notre Dame win for that.

The game went to two overtimes. UCLA squandered a comfortable lead in regulation time before the Wolfpack fought back to tie after forty minutes. They played even for one extra five-minute session. UCLA jumped seven points ahead in the second extra session, but big Burleson, high-leaping Thompson, and the others scrambled back and finally won, 80-77. Walton had played with his usual intensity and determination, scoring 29 points and adding 18 rebounds, but the opposition had played that much better a game and had earned the victory.

Walton neither pouted nor sulked. He even chatted with reporters briefly after the game, signed autographs on his way out of the building.

"We had the game in hand twice and then made critical mistakes," said Coach Wooden. "We took three shots we shouldn't have with the eleven-point lead [late in regulation time] and then made a couple of crucial mistakes in the second overtime. I knew our streak [of seven consecutive NCAA titles, 38 tournament victories without defeat] couldn't go on forever. I'm just happy we had the run we did. It was a great one. A lot of things broke right for us in a lot of ways . . . but they didn't today."

On March 25, N.C. State defeated Marquette for the NCAA championship, 76-61, and UCLA defeated Kansas for third place, 76-61. Walton completed his college career as UCLA's number two all-time leading scorer behind Alcindor, but surpassed his predecessor in rebounding with 1370 in his three varsity seasons and had a career field-goal-shooting percentage of .651, surpassing the NCAA record of .639 set originally by Alcindor.

It was disappointing that UCLA no longer ruled college basketball, but no one felt that the demise of the dynasty was Walton's fault. It was revealed that he had played since his shattering fall at Washington State with two chipped vertebrae. He had undergone additional acupuncture treatments so that he could play without having to resort to numbing drugs.

/ / /

Pain-relief treatment would have helped the professionals, too. Their agonizing over how to deal with Walton had continued through his final weeks as a Bruin. The NBA, faced with a decision which might have profound effect on its rivalry with the ABA, chose to abide by its long-standing draft procedure, no matter the risk. The ABA had San Diego prepared to offer Walton a contract, but was also willing to create a new franchise around him and even was ready to move the Carolina team to Los Angeles if that seemed the best pursuit to follow.

Only two days after the NCAA finals, NBA Commissioner J. Walter Kennedy presided at the coin-flip ceremony which had been so eagerly awaited for so long. Portland had finished with the worst record in the Western Conference, Philadelphia with the worst in the East for the second straight year. "Heads," called the 76ers. Tails the coin came up. Walton's NBA rights belonged to Portland.

Walton would be represented, as had most UCLA athletes before him, by contractor Gilbert and by attorney Ralph Shapiro, both acting on his behalf at no fee. Walton would not take part in discussions with money people himself. Instead, he asked his father to attend meetings as his spokesman, although it was agreed the final decision would belong to the boy.

"I tried to communicate how he feels," Ted Walton explained to the San Diego *Tribune*'s Bob Ortman shortly after negotiations with the four contending groups began. "Bill has certain firm ideas about where he wants to play, the kind of organization he wants to play with, and, of course, the way he wants to live. Overriding to him is the way to live. . . . We're not participating in an auction. One offer will be accepted from each league, and that will be it. The decision will be solely Bill's. He's a man. He has a mind of his own. I think many people have found that out."

The athlete fled from the bickering over contract details by taking a cycling trip down the rugged Baja California peninsula of Mexico. Before departing, he sought counsel from two friends—All-Pro Jerry West of the Lakers and ex-Bruin Sidney Wicks, alongside whom he would play if he chose to go to Portland.

The ABA offered $2.5 million, it later was learned, while Portland offered only $1.9 million, both contracts to be for five years. The thought of living in the quiet solitude of the Oregon wilderness and of playing in the more stable, more competitive NBA prevailed over the $600,000 difference.

"There were clauses we were capable of getting for Bill that perhaps we couldn't get for another player," Gilbert revealed. "Before he could be traded, for instance, the trade would have to have his approval. That's a very important item, in view of Bill's life style. Another thing he requested is that, when he's interviewed, he be allowed to say what he feels and not what someone tells him to say."

On the same trip to Portland on which he formally signed his contract and went through the obligatory postsigning news conference, Walton began to build his adult life. First, he purchased a tract of land in the suburb of West Linn, bordering the Willamette River. Second, he bought himself a new lumberjack-style plaid shirt to wear with his well-worn jeans. He wanted to grow vegetables on his land, he said.

He returned to Southern California to begin enjoying, with a modesty true to his philosophy, some of the benefits of his new income. He traded in the tired little Toyota sedan he'd driven since his sophomore season and purchased a new car . . . a gas-saving compact rather than the luxurious Lincoln or Cadillac favored by other young men following their first pro contracts. On a brief visit with his parents in La Mesa in early June, his Wooden-imposed short haircut having grown into a lengthening shag and his strong chin hidden under a new beard, Walton spoke in favor of a local school-bond issue. He added, "I want to play pro basketball, and I want to keep my private life private as much as possible."

Portland's team orthopedic specialist, Dr. Frank Smith, had recommended surgery to remove chips of loose cartilage in Walton's left knee before his rookie season began. The operation was called "minor," but Walton laughed at that descrip-

tion. "It's always minor," he snorted, "when it's on someone
else."

/ / /

The professional glory which seemed inevitable for Walton,
as great as he had been at UCLA, was slow in coming. He
turned to strict vegetarianism in the summer following the
surgery, and his weight fell from 235 pounds to less than 215.
In Portland's preseason workouts and early exhibition games,
he played with maturity and cleverness. It seemed certain that
he would vindicate those who promised professional greatness
for him, although some observers did believe him too eccentric to withstand the physical and mental rigors of professional
life.

Although he had promised the Trail Blazers' management
his weight would increase once two-a-day workouts ended and
the season began, he remained gaunt-featured and was
occasionally overpowered by rival, less talented giants. In
November, he sustained a hand injury, and he complained of
a pain in his heel which was diagnosed as a bone spur . . . a
trivial, yet painful, ailment accepted by many athletes as an
occupational hazard.

From the first game he missed because of injury through
the rest of the season, Walton was notable in the NBA for his
absences and reticence rather than for his athletic accomplishments. He severed his friendship with Gilbert and turned for
legal assistance to Charles Garry, a San Francisco attorney
noted for his eloquent defense of radicals and revolutionists
including Eldrige Cleaver and Huey Newton, leaders of the
Black Panther Party. Walton was said, further, to have resisted
requests by Portland team physicians that he accept medical
treatment involving widely used anti-inflammatory and pain-
killing drugs. He feared risk of aggravated injury which might
impair his health later in life, he insisted. There was another
shock: it was learned that people whom he had befriended
and even invited into his West Linn home as temporary
residents, Jack and Mickie Scott, were involved in the continued flight from custody of publishing heiress Patricia
Hearst.

While Portland finished a disappointing third in the Pacific

Division and rumors circulated about a possible trade which might send him on to another team, Walton remained in seclusion, recovering from his ailments and emerging now and then for a television appearance or a newspaper interview. Mostly, he talked politics and about the Scotts and his brief relationship with the FBI, offering convincing evidence that the Federal agency had either tapped his phone or conducted some sort of surveillance on him, as he had claimed.

In an interview with Bill McFarland of the Portland bureau of United Press International in late May, he said, "I find it very difficult to understand why I'm called controversial. I try to be straightforward, tell the truth, and express myself from conviction. Most of my views are straight down the line, even those off the basketball court. I'm only twenty-two, and that is a young age for a professional athlete. I am looking forward to a long career in the NBA. I love basketball. I love to play it, and I plan to play it for a long time. I think I can help the Portland Trail Blazers. I believe they think I can be an asset to the team. . . . The people in Portland and the fans in the NBA have not yet seen me play my best basketball, but they must remember I have been hurt."

Several days after that interview, a final judgment was delivered by his UCLA days' coach. "Some of the things Bill has done," said John Wooden at a clinic appearance in Massachussetts, "have been horrible. I am critical of them and so should you be." The newly retired coach continued, "Bill is intensely interested in his fellow man. But he follows anyone with a new idea. Give me two hours alone with Bill and I will get him on the right track. The trouble is, give some other guy two hours after me and Bill's gone again."

The Gym Rats were bored with Walton by then, anyway. They were surveying the colleges and high schools, looking for new names and faces to follow.

In Walton's senior class of collegians, there had been half a dozen players drafted by the professionals in the hope they'd emerge as effective centers the way Dave Cowens had blossomed once he got into the NBA.

North Carolina State's Burleson, at 7-4, was the tallest of the country's players, college or pro, but there were serious doubts about his strength and stamina. He was drafted by Bill

Russell and the Seattle Sonics, perhaps because of a feeling that Caucasian youngsters [Walton an exception] tend to mature slowly. Russell would be content to wait and to work with Burleson, and his patience proved fruitful as the gaunt youngster developed through a promising rookie season.

There were no Waltons in the junior and sophomore classes, but there were at least two dozen men in the 6-foot-10 to 7-foot-2 range who had ambitions of becoming their senior year's most sought-after big man.

At little Morgan State in Maryland, 6-foot-11 Marvin Webster, a product of Baltimore, earned the nickname "the Human Eraser" because his play around the basket wiped out his teammates' defensive mistakes so often. He led his division's rebounders with an average of 22.4 per game while blocking 249 shots. The Utah Stars of the ABA wanted him badly after his sophomore season, but he chose to remain in college rather than sign. "I knew I wasn't ready to play pro ball," he said. "I have to polish up my game more, put on a little more weight, and get my hook shot down. Money isn't everything. I like Morgan and I want to finish school."

True to his word, he refused to apply for hardship status in the NBA draft following his junior season despite pressures. He would have been drafted early in the proceedings if he had been willing to forgo his diploma. An illness, hepatitis, struck him the next summer and, as he recovered, his weight zoomed past 250 pounds. He started his senior season slowly, but finished strongly to lead Morgan State to an NCAA championship, and was drafted number three among all collegians the next May by the Atlanta Hawks, fulfilling his role as "best big man available."

On the West Coast there was another prominent 7-footer at Stanford, Rich Kelley, whom pro scouts were watching. He came from the exclusive community of Woodside and had played at Menlo Park High in one of the Bay Area's most favored communities. He was uncomplicated and likable . . . if anything, too calm, too unruffled. He had a feathery shooting touch and had played on U.S. National teams in the Soviet Union one summer and in Red China prior to his senior season. Stanford Coach Howie Dallmar fought hard to see him recognized as second in the powerful Pac-8 Conference only to Walton in his junior season, as best big man when he was a senior. The New Orleans Jazz agreed, apparently, for they made him their number-one draft choice.

Washington State Coach George Raveling challenged Dallmar's claims on behalf of Kelley. His nominee was Steve Puidokas, a 6-foot-11½ youngster from St. Laurence High in Chicago who emulated the great George Mikan not only in his Illinois origins, but also in his heft at 258 pounds and his inside strength. Raveling claimed Puidokas would be the country's best big man by the time he was a senior, and people who had to battle against him tended to give those claims respect.

/ / /

None of the collegians was as exciting to the pro scouts and to the basketball underground as Moses Malone. Here was a player to ignite the imagination and send the Gym Rats scurrying to the out-of-town newspaper stands to bone up on his statistics and credentials.

First there was his size. As a high-school senior at Petersburg, Virginia, he was already 6-foot-11 and 220 pounds. Then there was his name—*Moses Malone*. How deliciously superstar-like and melodious! If his skills could carry it, he'd certainly *sound* right as a great young star. "The Big M," certainly he'd be called. He could be, like Isaac Hayes, a great *Black Moses*. Malone led Petersburg High to the Virginia State championship in his junior season, but blossomed even more prominently in 1973–74. He averaged 38.8 points per game, averaged better than 20 rebounds a night, and averaged more than 12 blocked shots even though he was playing only eight-minute high-school periods. "A lot of people," said the schoolboy as scores of scholarship offers began to pour in, "tell me I'm the best, that I'm the greatest that ever played the game. But me? I'm just another player."

Malone's exploits circulated swiftly among the Gym Rats in December and January. He was listed in all the preseason magazines. Predictably, by March, after leading Petersburg to a 25-0 season and another state title, he was the subject of national magazine stories and of lengthy features carried nationally by AP and UPI.

"People tell me how much money I might be worth right

The country's most sought-after high-school basketball player of 1974, Moses Malone, chats with two of Petersburg, Virginia, High School's cutest coeds . . . and a news photographer is there to record it. It was national news a few weeks later when he accepted a scholarship to the University of Maryland

now," he said in one of the flurry of interviews. "I really don't think about the money, not now. I've got too much basketball to play, gotta learn more about the game."

The college scholarship offers continued to pour in and the reporters continued to cluster around him as he went to Pittsburgh in late March to play in the annual Roundball Classic, considered to be the most important of several national high-school all-star games played each spring. He had college coaches panting even more hungrily after him following the game than before it as he scored 31 points and hauled down 20 rebounds. He capped a Most Valuable Player performance by scoring the winning field goal for the United States All-Stars against the all-Pennsylvania team with a thunderous slam dunk goal only nine seconds before the final buzzer.

It is obligatory that an emerging great big man be hailed as soon as he reaches a certain degree of fame as "ready to play right now against . . ." For Abdul-Jabbar, the comparisons were with Russell and Wilt Chamberlain. For Walton, the comparisons were with Abdul-Jabbar. For Malone, the standard of brilliance was Walton.

The recruiting sweepstakes intensified through spring and into early summer. The University of New Mexico stationed an assistant coach in a motel outside of Petersburg for fully three months, attempting to convince the boy and his widowed mother of the merits of an education in the Southwest. Finally, as rumors circulated about alleged irregularities and of inducements offered which were in violation of NCAA recruiting codes, Malone announced that he had chosen to attend Driesell's school, the University of Maryland. Reports came of an NCAA investigation, and Malone posed happily for a national magazine alongside a new Chrysler Imperial he'd purchased on a long-term loan payable when he would eventually turn pro. An insurance policy was also financed on a future basis, guaranteeing the boy $1 million, it was reported, should he be injured in college play and have to forgo a pro career. And Maryland, as early as July, was being ranked number one in the country because the Terps could boast so great a young center. Pro basketball interfered. Malone never played for Maryland. Instead, he was pursued with renewed vigor in September by the Utah Stars and agreed, after four days of nationally publicized negotiations, to go directly from high school into the ABA. It was a distasteful thing to see, those of us who knew a less competitive and less lucrative basketball era felt, but Malone and the Stars were within their legal rights. They were vindicated to a degree when, at nineteen, Moses became a leading Rookie of the Year candidate. Few Americans were unfamiliar with Malone's name in September of 1974. A year later, he was a national celebrity—dramatic proof of the way basketball fame's old development process has accelerated.

/ / /

UCLA, fallen from the national throne in the loss to North Carolina State, wasn't ready to concede that its nontitle status had to be long-lasting. Behind Walton, Coach Wooden already had been grooming 7-foot-0 junior Ralph Drollinger, like Walton a graduate of a San Diego area high school (Grossmont), and behind Drollinger was freshman Richard Washington, 6-foot-9, who had starred the previous season for Benson Tech of Portland.

They were not superstars like Alcindor or Walton before them. But they were coachable and eager, and they were the NCAA title-game heroes as Coach Wooden closed an incredible coaching career, to be succeeded by Gene Bartow, with a victory over the University of Kentucky which gave UCLA its tenth crown in twelve years.

UCLA was represented on the All-American teams in 1974–75 not by a center, but by a forward, Dave Meyers. There *was* no dominating center in NCAA major college ranks that season. But that didn't mean great centers were out of the news. The talk among the Gym Rats and college recruiters was that a new blue chipper had emerged—a 7-foot-1½ undergrad at little Elk Grove High near Sacramento, California, named Bill Cartwright.

The man who developed him and guided him, Coach Dan Risley, reported breathlessly, "People who have seen Moses Malone say Billy is much better. Billy can shoot from twenty feet out, he puts the ball on the floor, can drive the lane either left or right, hooks left or right . . . he's truly gifted. And he's a tremendous young man with an unbelievably good attitude. He realizes that, with his potential plus hard work, he could be on top of the world."

In both his junior and senior seasons, Cartwright over-powered opponents as Elk Grove won sectional champion-ships. In 1975, Elk Grove went on to capture northern California's most important high-school event, too, the Tournament of Champions, before nearly 13,000 fans at Oakland Coliseum-Arena. He was pursued for interviews by newspaper, magazine, and television reporters, but was spared intense recruiting during the second half of his senior season because he announced as early as January that he would accept a scholarship from the University of San Francisco . . . the school first thrust into prominence by a fellow named Bill Russell.

Cartwright's early disclosure, following his first buzz of national notoriety the year before, brought attention to a remarkable group of high-school seniors, each of whom was being acclaimed in his own community as a future challenger not only of Cartwright but also, naturally, of Malone . . . Walton . . . Abdul-Jabbar.

In Southern California, 6-foot-11 David Greenwood of Verbum Dei High (Los Angeles) was called the best prep since Walton. He led his team to an undefeated season marred in the sectional championships by an upset loss to Palos Verdes High. After that game, the Palos Verdes rooters hailed their own man—Bill Laimbeer, 6-foot-11, a soft-shooting young Goliath similar to Stanford's Kelley in background in that his school was located in a plush suburb, a contrast to Verbum Dei's inner-city location.

The East Coast had its young marvels, too—Larry Gibson of Baltimore's Dunbar High, a 6-foot-10½ shot-blocking whiz; Bernard Toone of Gorton High in Yonkers, New York, a 6-foot-9 scrapper who outplayed Cartwright in a couple of postseason all-star games; and a muscular youngster from Maynard Evens High in Orlando, Florida, Darryle Dawkins, 6-foot-10, who was acclaimed as the best in his state since Artis Gilmore's years at Jacksonville State.

With so rich a harvest, little wonder that college coaches and professional scouts defied their budgets and a shaky

Bill Nichols, San Francisco Examiner

Elk Grove High's Bill Cartwright soars to rim height to score from point-blank range for a school he helped make supreme in Northern California

national economy by setting all-time records for cross-country travel and cross-country ambition. Maryland, frustrated earlier at the loss of Malone, was rewarded when Gibson elected to remain in his home state. Laimbeer, his parents having moved to Toledo for professional reasons, bypassed West Coast scholarship offers to join Coach Digger Phelps at Notre Dame. Greenwood decided to help perpetuate the UCLA dynasty and was joined as a Westwood freshman by two brilliant backcourt prospects, teammate and long-time buddy Roy Hamilton of Verbum Dei and Brad Holland of La Crescenta High. The UCLA coup was acclaimed as the greatest harvest for a school since the Lew Alcindor–Lucius Allen–Lynn Shackelford group of nearly a decade earlier.

The surprise was Dawkins. The Philadelphia 76ers, continuing to yearn for greatness at center and frustrated earlier in their pursuit of Walton, decided to gamble on the Florida youngster and offered him $1 million over a seven-year contract to bypass college ball in favor of a jump directly to the pros. He was the first high-school boy ever drafted by the older league, and the knowledgeable Jack McMahon, the club's director of player personnel, explained, "Darryle just doesn't look like a high-school player to me. He's as talented as any player I've ever seen."

There were equally promising forwards and guards abounding in American high schools (including 6-foot-8 Bill Willoughby of Dwight Morrow High in Engelwood, N.J., drafted by Atlanta on the second round as the NBA's second prep draftee), but the grand prizes in the recruiting wars went to the schools and the pros with the most dominating centers. The more things change, a philosopher noted once, the more they stay the same. And another philosopher, NBA variety, noted, "You can't teach a kid to be seven feet tall."

12

EPILOGUE: WAYNE MCKOY

Always, somewhere, there is a young giant growing to maturity who threatens to obliterate all the accomplishments of even the greatest basketball players who came before him. The cycle is a joy for those who follow the game, but it can be agony for the boys who become the young men who become the fading veterans who play it.

Wayne McKoy weighed 235 pounds and stretched 6-foot-8 by the time he was fifteen years old. He was abandoned by his parents in North Carolina and raised by an aunt who brought him to Long Island when he was four years old. He could not adjust to public school because streetwise boys shorter than he taunted and fought with him because he was so big, therefore so alien. Before he could legally drive an automobile or even begin to think about college, he was prominent in the files of basketball coaches and professional scouts. Already, interview requests had to be screened and college coaches had to be told to leave him alone, lest he have no time to study or to mature into his size.

"We think Wayne is far advanced over Lew Alcindor at a comparable stage," said the Reverend Ed Visscher, coach at

Long Island Lutheran High School of Brookville, New York, in the winter of 1974. "By the end of his sophomore season, we want Wayne to be as good as Alcindor was when he graduated from high school. By the end of his senior year, we want him to be as good as Alcindor was when he graduated college. And we think he will be."

Coach Digger Phelps of Notre Dame knows about McKoy, and knows that many other coaches do, too. "It's a shame," he told Tony Kornheiser of Long Island's *Newsday.* "He has to face four years of recruiting when most kids only have to face one. Lew Alcindor is the greatest example. He was recruited for four years, too. He was really a lonely kid. I hope it doesn't happen to this one, too."

The boy recalled circumstances which forced him out of public grammar school and into a parochial school (Lutheran Redeemer of Long Island) as early as the third grade. "I had problems," he said. "I was treated unfairly. Kids used to try to beat me up, and whenever I hit back I got yelled at. People called me a big dummy all the time. It really hurt me."

The Reverend Visscher met the boy two years after he entered Lutheran Redeemer. The boy stood 6-foot-4 then. "I was there to deliver a lecture," Visscher recalled, "and I told Wayne to remember me."

When McKoy was ready to enter high school, he chose Lutheran because of the earlier meeting with the Reverend Visscher and because of the advice of one of his teachers, who happened to have been a college classmate of the minister-coach. There was no scholarship available for the boy, but tuition was raised through a City League scholarship fund grant, through the donation of a high-school teacher who demanded anonymity for his philanthropy, through funds provided by his aunt (Mrs. Beatrice Wooten), and through work offered McKoy as a part-time custodian for the school gym. The Reverend Visscher, noting the boy's promise and his need, invited McKoy to live with him and his family of five children along with two other members of the team.

"Things aren't so bad," said McKoy earnestly. "Most people are friendly. In school I'm just another guy. Everyone is my friend. At least they seem to be. Being tall hasn't been a problem yet. I have a girl friend. And I don't hang out much with older guys. My best friend is only fourteen. His name is Rocky. He's small. I guess the only time I wish I was smaller is when I see all the clothes he has and I can't fit into them."

As a ninth-grader, McKoy became the key player for a team ranked best in the state outside of New York City. The pressure was building on him already, even though the team included a more polished, older player, Reggie Carter, who lived with the Visscher family, too.

"Reggie's my best player," said the coach, "but I can't get anyone to pay attention to him. It's grossly unfair, but Wayne is going to get most of the attention. I learned a lot from the Lew Alcindor–Jack Donohue era at Power Memorial. I thought Lew never learned—except by withdrawal—to deal with the press. I'm going to expose Wayne to the media gradually. I don't want him to withdraw. But he has to learn that people are going to make a fuss over him. Actually, I told him I felt sorry for him. He won't be able to lead a normal life."

"I feel bad when people only want to talk to me," said the teen-ager, "so I don't ever brag about the stories about me. If I bragged, I might lose my friends. I don't need people to dislike me. Without friends . . . that'd be really bad."

Wayne McKoy. Age 15. Lionized and sought-after and cheered during the game. . . . Fighting to remain an individual, eager to be accepted by the group, reduced to sweeping the gym in the quiet long after the battle.

The details of his life are different in the specifics, but his story is one with Lew Alcindor's and Wilt Chamberlain's and Bill Russell's and George Mikan's and, it's rational to presume, with the Biblical Goliath's. Wayne McKoy's size and strength and growing basketball skill make him a hero. Yet his height sets him apart and insures that he'll face trauma and despair in his life as often as he experiences joy. In time, he probably will become wealthy. But he will pay a heavy price.

If he is fortunate—and thus far he has been—he will find a way to cope with his life and with the people around him. He will have to live as a giant, as a black man, as a public figure.

He may choose pride and insight as did Bill Russell, or personal indulgence and luxury as did Wilt Chamberlain, or religious conviction as have Kareem Abdul-Jabbar and Elvin Hayes.

Failing, he will retire into the murk along with Gene Wiley, Billy McGill, Jim McDaniels, and the nameless thousands of other tall young men who flirted with success and floundered. There will be many hands reaching out to help him, but just as many ready to drag him downward to despair.

This is the life we offer to the giants, surveying them one by one, discarding them, and searching further for those younger, stronger, taller who will fight our fights for us and whose glory we may vicariously share. There is nothing we withhold from those who meet our standards of achievement, and there is little we offer to those who fail.

"Fee, fi, fo, fum," says the giant, and we shiver at the majesty of his power.

"I shall slay the giant," says daring young Jack . . . and when the giant has fallen, we hail Jack for his deed.